UPANISHADS, GĪTĀ AND BIBLE

UPANISHADS
GĪTĀ AND BIBLE

A Comparative Study
of Hindu and Christian Scriptures

by

GEOFFREY PARRINDER

Professor of the Comparative Study of Religions
in the University of London

HARPER TORCHBOOKS

Harper & Row, Publishers

New York, Evanston, San Francisco, London

This book was first published in 1962 by Faber and Faber Limited, London and is here reprinted by arrangement.

First HARPER TORCHBOOK edition published 1972

LIBRARY OF CONGRESS CATALOG CARD NUMBER: 72–188029

STANDARD BOOK NUMBER: 06–131660–1

CONTENTS

CONTENTS

Chapter 1

INTRODUCTION

The religions of the world are in closer contact today than ever before in history. Until the nineteenth century they were isolated from each other, by geographical barriers and by the lack of knowledge of religions shown by most of the travellers who went east and west. The Indian Upanishads were only first and partially translated into English from Sanskrit in 1832, and only adequately from 1884. Since then many other texts have been published of numerous Indian classics, and cheap and reliable versions are available to the public. In the same period, the Bible has been translated into over two hundred languages, and parts of it into nearly a thousand, and the Christian scriptures are known and studied in many eastern lands.

With the close communications of today, and the easy accessibility of the sacred scriptures, the religions of the world can no longer afford to ignore each other's teachings. In the West many eastern ideas have become known: *karma*, *yoga* and *nirvāṇa* are referred to in our literature and have found their way into English dictionaries. The *Brahman* and the *ātman* have not quite arrived there but are in fairly common currency. One inevitable result is that there is a great deal of loose and ill-informed treatment of eastern concepts, and they tend to be regarded as almost interchangeable with Christian beliefs, the *Brahman* being likened to God and *nirvāṇa* to an oriental heaven.

Quite apart from the occultist who delights in the mysterious and the half-understood, there are many others who feel that all religions are the same, or have some kind of transcendent unity.

This tendency is even more characteristic of modern India. Differently from the past, when the Upanishads were secrets jealously guarded by the Brahmins, today all mysteries are to be uncovered and all declared the same. All religions are equal, but 'some are more equal than others' if they recognize this claim. Gone is the *odium theologicum*, says a friend, half-regretfully.

An unfortunate result of careless mingling of beliefs is that those who hold firmly to one religion, but might be induced to take an interest in others, are repelled by this attempt at ironing out differences as if they did not matter. But the differences between religions may be as significant as their similarities. It is important therefore that when comparisons are made, as they are today willy-nilly, they should be careful and informed, and guided by as full a knowledge of the facts as possible.

Some religions are close to one another, in history and teaching: for example, Christianity, Judaism and Islam on the one hand, or Hinduism and Buddhism on the other. But there is a great divide between Christianity and Hinduism. As Professor R. C. Zaehner has said, 'When we look at the religions of the world, we are faced with two totally different approaches to the whole subject, we are faced with two chosen peoples, not one; for, whereas Europe and the Near East owe their religions directly or indirectly to the Jews, further Asia owes hers directly or indirectly to the Indians.'[1]

The Semitic and the Indian are the two main streams of religious thought. They are very different from one another, having arisen in dissimilar surroundings and following varying courses. Yet, despite their unlikeness, these religions are now in contact and need mutual interpretation. Whether they are compatible or not, and opinions will diverge on this, the encounter of religions is taking place and is one of the most important events of our time.

The chapters which follow are an attempt at interpreting some of the major teachings of the classical scriptures of Hinduism and Christianity. Hinduism was selected as the fount from which other Indian religions took their rise, and within Hinduism that classical part of it which used to be called Brahmanism. There are countless religious writings in India, but all Hindus recognize as authoritative scriptures the Veda and Vedānta, that is to say, the ancient Vedic hymns and the early Upanishads. These are *śruti*, inspired words 'heard' by the ancient seers, and distinguished from the later *smṛiti*, 'remembered' texts. The long line of Indian thinkers, stretching at least three thousand years, could not all be considered in a short study, and so the classical Vedānta was chosen as that upon which later developments rest.

The name Veda, 'knowledge', is given to the most ancient texts of Indian religion, principally the hymns of the Ṛig Veda. Vedānta means the 'end of the Veda', or the highest peak and complete knowledge of Vedic teaching. Strictly Vedānta is first applied to the Upanishads, 'secret teachings', which are the basis of Hindu religious philosophy. The word is also used to describe later philosophies and even some modern Hindu teachings. Here we shall keep to the oldest usage. The only later text that will be referred to much apart from the Upanishads is the Bhagavad Gītā, the 'Song of the Lord'. Although not nominally in the same class, the Gītā has been linked with the Upanishads for many centuries and many Hindus regard it as inspired *śruti*.

Among the religions of Semitic origin Christianity was chosen for comparison, as the religion of the majority of those who are likely to read this book, or at least best known to the West. Once again there is a long line of Christian thinkers and many later doctrinal developments, and so the Bible, both Old and New Testaments, was taken because of its fundamental teachings of God and man. Its authority is determinative for all later Christian teaching. The Bible is the scripture of all Christian churches, the religious classic of the West.

Juxtaposition of Hindu and Christian teaching can be casual and superficial, but done seriously and in detail there is evidence that it meets a real need. If it reveals that the Biblical world is almost entirely different from the Vedāntic it may serve a purpose. On the other hand, it may also show that there is mutual concern, if not agreement, about many of the great themes of life and death and eternity.

This is an essay in the comparative study of religions, and certain possible criticisms must be met. There are those who maintain that no comparisons are possible, even between peas in a pod, although everybody does compare them.[2] But more seriously it may well be asked whether two religions as unlike as Christianity and Hinduism can be compared. And the short answer is that this is being done every day. Missionaries compare their own faith with others, usually to the detriment of the other. And syncretism and mingling of beliefs are characteristic of today, and practised widely in India and Europe. In Christianity Jewish and Greek ideas have long been mixed. Some regret this and would even now cry, 'Thy sons, O Zion, against thy sons, O Greece.'[3] But the process cannot be reversed. In our time new enrichment is coming to the West from India and, since the Indian tradition is so much more religious than the Greek, it is 'more natural for us' to look for religious kinship 'not so much among the Greeks as among the nations of Asia; for it is Asia that is the birthplace of every single religion that has withstood the test of time'.[4]

It may also be asked whether the Upanishads and the Bible can be seriously compared, since the first is philosophy and the second religion. But Indian philosophy is nearly always religious, and while it is not usually biographical it deals with problems that are fundamental to religion. It treats of 'human being, eternity and God'. The immortality of the soul which, it is said, has not been considered by the dominant Oxford schools of philosophy these thirty years, is believed in by all religions and is axiomatic to the Upanishads. Moreover, differently from much Greek and later European philosophy, Indian thought is based on experience, and this will appear in its conceptions of God and particularly in its approach to mysticism. On the other hand, the Bible is not without its speculations and, for example, on the universal problem of suffering its questionings are much more persistent than those of the Upanishads. But these are variations that will appear in the course of this study and if in fact the two bodies of scripture, the Indian and the Jewish, are incompatible then we must say so. At least such a negative answer would be one reason for making clear what the distinctive or even 'unique' points of each religion are.

Then it may be asked whether the comparison goes far enough. And it must be confessed that restriction of the study to the Upanishads and the Bhagavad Gītā inevitably leaves out some features of later Hinduism. For example the chief deities of modern India, Śiva and the Great Mother, find no mention here, and Vishṇu only as he appears in the guise of Kṛishṇa in the Bhagavad Gītā. Yet this is a study of the classical scriptures and must stick to its subject, and it is hoped to deal with the main teachings adequately.

On the other hand some of the cardinal Biblical doctrines will be mentioned but not fully treated, for example, the incarnation and the atonement. That may be attempted some other time, but the aim of the present book is primarily to give an idea of the Upanishads to Europeans, and to show Indians where the more significant parallels and variants are in the Bible. It is not a book of apologetic, either Vedāntic or Biblical, and it aims at strict impartiality. Perhaps some day a new study will be made of Christian doctrine in the light of Indian thought; but that time has hardly come yet, for we are not prepared either with enough knowledge of Hinduism, or with the courage to reopen the old Christological controversies.

To place the Upanishads and the Bible in close confrontation is a kind of religious dialogue. But dialogue can be conducted in a number of ways. The old method was that of propaganda, singling out some idea, stating it imperfectly, and then refuting it with the weight of a contrary tradition. Another manner is the Socratic question and answer, but this can become scrappy and confusing. What will be done here will allow each religion to speak for itself. The Upanishadic passages will be given first on each subject, and the Biblical parallels or differences will follow, shorter but in so far as they can reasonably be called into account.

What is attempted is to present a clear and fair picture of some of the great doctrines of the Hindu classics, and put them alongside classical Christian teachings on similar topics. This is done for the use of those who are interested in the modern encounter of religions. I have pored over the Upanishads and the Bhagavad Gītā for years and have sought the best rendering of words and texts, but my chief concern is with the large themes of teaching and I have leant heavily on the works of Hume, Radhakrishnan, Dasgupta, Keith and Zimmer on the Upanishads. By placing the scriptures side by side, and letting them speak for themselves without judgement or effort to prove the superiority of one or the other, it is hoped that light will be shed upon some of the great religious problems with which the mind of man has been concerned, at many times and in many places.

A prefatory word must be said on the character of the Veda and Vedānta. The collection of hymns which forms the Ṛig Veda is the oldest source of texts on Indian religion, begun perhaps before 1000 B.C. but passed on orally and not written down till much later. The Upanishads ('sitting down near' or 'secret sessions') are discourses and dialogues of which the oldest were compiled perhaps between 800 and 500 B.C., though the dating depends partly upon the traditional dates of Buddhism and Jainism, and these may have to be modified in the light of archaeological discovery. In any case, the Upanishads, the 'end of the Vedas', the true Vedānta, are a growth over a long period and contain magical ideas along with profound speculations.

The Upanishads are varied and not systematic; they present diverse views, just as the Bible does. Later philosophers sought to interpret all the Upanishads to fit in with their brand of doctrine, but this does violence to the heterogeneity of Upanishadic thought. Professor Dasgupta warns us to 'turn a deaf ear to the absolute claims of these exponents, and look upon the Upaniṣads not as a systematic treatise but as a repository of diverse currents of thought—the melting pot in which all later philosophic ideas were still in a state of confusion'. The later non-dualistic philosophy of Śaṅkara appropriated the term Vedānta to itself, and today Vedānta is often regarded as identical with non-dualist or monist thought. But 'there are many other systems which put forth their claim as representing the true Vedānta doctrines'.[5]

The Bhagavad Gītā is rather later, perhaps to be dated about the turn of the Christian era. Its teaching again is a fusion of several strands, but the strong theism that emerges reinforced one important line of Hindu thought, and this provides a most valuable point of comparison with other theistic religions.

There are over a hundred extant Upanishads, some of comparatively recent formation; but the oldest and classical works are generally reckoned at thirteen and to these almost alone will reference be made here. The earliest, the Bṛihad-āraṇyaka and the Chāndogya Upanishads, contain some sacrificial discussions that link up with the priestly Brāhmaṇas which came between the Vedic hymns and the Upanishads, but they contain many of the germs also of later Hindu doctrines. The Taittirīya and Aitareya Upanishads probably came next, to be followed by the Kaushītaki and the Kena which is partly in verse. The next group is mostly in verse: the Kaṭha, Īśa, Muṇḍaka and Śvetāśvatara Upanishads; it is here that the development of theism appears. Finally come more prose Upanishads: Praśna, Maitri and Māṇḍūkya. With this sketch of the order we may now proceed to discuss their teaching.

These chapters were first prepared at the request of the University of London Extra-Mural department, and delivered at the London headquarters of the World Congress of Faiths at Younghusband House. Then the Oxford University Extra-Mural delegacy asked for a repetition of the lectures at their centre at Brighton and this allowed for revision and expansion. Both audiences were mixed, comprising Christians, Hindus, Buddhists and Muslims. The lively discussion that followed each lecture showed that the subject was of topical interest and requests were made for publication. I am grateful to these and other friends for their interest and stimulating argument. I wish to express my thanks also to Professor R. C. Zaehner of Oxford, and to Professor H. D. Lewis of London, for reading the book in manuscript and making most valuable suggestions.

References

1. *At Sundry Times* (Faber & Faber, 1958), p. 16.
2. See also my *Comparative Religion* (Allen & Unwin, 1962), p. 11.
3. Zechariah 9, 13.
4. *At Sundry Times*, pp. 165 f.
5. *A History of Indian Philosophy* (Cambridge, 1922), vol. i, p. 42.

Chapter 2

IN THE BEGINNING

The origins of the world and man are of interest to most religions. 'In the beginning', they say. This phrase is common to both Vedānta and the Bible, and the Indian thinkers had an even greater curiosity than the Hebrews about the origin of things. In the beginning, we read in the Upanishads, the world was non-existent, there was nothing here at all; or all this was Brahman, one only; or the world was but the soul (*ātman*), the soul alone was this.[1]

The ancient Indian sages were not afraid of asking questions. Like the elephant's child in *Just So Stories* they were full of insatiable curiosity, a feature of Indian life that has remained to this day. The title of the Praśna Upanishad means 'question' (*praśna*), and in its six sections six inquirers ask the sage Pippalāda: Whence are creatures born? which is the chief sustaining power? how does life come into and leave the body? what is sleep and the basis of things? what world is won by meditation? how does individuality merge into unity? Similarly the Kena Upanishad takes its name from the questions with which it starts: By whom (*kena*) directed does the mind soar up? by whom does breath come forth? by whose will does speech appear? by what god are ear and eye prompted?

This restless inquiry into the universe continues: What is its cause? where do men come from? how do they live? is it time, necessity, nature or chance? Then how does the soul exist?[2] Questions about the creation of the world and man are constantly recurring, and many possibilities are considered. Often the problems go on in a long series, connected by 'ask me another', or 'instruct me still further'. Although touched on already in the earlier Vedic texts, speculation about the origins of the universe had not grown old in Vedāntic times and, as a modern commentator asks, 'When will it?'

Already towards the close of the hymns of the Ṛig Veda, the most ancient Indian texts, the early and rather barbaric Aryan warrior songs give way to deeper probings. The All-Maker (Viśvakarman), who had eyes and limbs on all sides, produced the heavens and the earth by his mighty power and without a companion. Or again, the Lord of Creatures (Prajāpati) alone comprehended all things, and the Golden Seed (Hiraṇyagarbha) arose in the beginning as lord of all creation to fix and uphold earth and heaven. Elsewhere, the Lord of Prayer (Brahmaṇaspati) is said to have forged everything together like a smith. And in a famous Hymn of Man (Purusha Sūkta) the thousand-membered primeval giant is sacrificed by the gods and of his different parts the world and men were made: the moon from his mind, the sun from his eye, gods from his mouth and breath, and also the four castes of men: Brahmins from his mouth, warriors from his arms, merchants from his thighs, menials from his feet. This conception appears in later writings, in the Upanishads and in the Laws of Manu.[3]

Out of these polytheistic and mythical notions there emerged at the end of the Ṛig Veda more profound speculations in the Song of Creation. Originally there was nothing but darkness, undistinguished chaos, without form and void. Then there was neither existence nor non-existence, and so the existent (*sat*) emerged from the non-existent (*asat*). No one can tell the origins of the creation. The very gods are later than the production of the world. Who then can know about it? He who looks on from the highest heaven, he knows, or perhaps even he does not know![4]

The concept of a primitive nothingness is criticized later. In the beginning the universe was neither non-existent nor existent, but Mind was there, and Mind was beyond existence. Pure nihilism appears to be an affront to the intelligence, and in the Upanishads the seer Uddālaka tells his son Śvetaketu that some people think that in the beginning there was Non-being only, without a second. But how could this be? How could Being be produced from Non-being? On the contrary, in the beginning there was Being alone.[5]

The idea of a Self-existent Being (Svayambhū) proved attractive. He is all-pervading and distributes objects eternally. In the later Laws of Manu the divine and indiscernible Self-existent made the rest of things appear by irresistible power. With a thought he created waters and placed his seed therein which became a golden egg (Hiraṇyagarbha) in which he himself was born as Brahman.

The myth of a cosmic egg appears several times in the Upanishads. In the beginning the world was non-existent but became somehow existent; it grew and turned into an egg and after a year burst open to reveal two parts, one silver which was the earth and the other gold which was the sky. This golden seed or egg, Hiraṇyagarbha, inherited from the Vedas, appears later with a personal creator who fashions the world.[6]

The Hymn of Creation said that water existed in the primeval darkness and that which came into being arose through heat. The potency of water is stressed again in the early Upanishads; in the beginning this world was just water, which produced the divine power Brahman, which produced the Lord of Creation (Prajāpati), who produced the gods. Prajāpati emerges as the creator who makes matter and life, the gods, man and woman, and the demons. He produced the world as food for himself, and taught the wisdom of the self both to the great god Indra and to the demon Virochana.

It will be seen that there are many rival theories, and no single or systematic development. But important and dominating ideas appear in the soul and Brahman. The soul (*ātman*) is said to have existed alone in the beginning. It was born through austerity out of the waters, brooded over them, separated out a form like an egg, entered into the secret place of the heart and looked out through beings. As in Plato's myth of the man-woman, so the soul was first alone and then divided into two: as man and wife, bull and cow, ram and ewe, and all paired things. Hence the undifferentiated universe became distinct in name and form (*nāma-rūpa*). But the soul remains invisible, like a razor in a case or fire in a holder.[7]

Relatively little detail is given of the process of creation, for the energies of the Upanishadic thinkers were turned to discovering the unifying principle behind and within all things. If this was not expressed as the soul (*ātman*), then it was the Holy Power (*brahman*), and indeed this latter neutral force came to predominate. In the beginning, all this was Brahman, it knew itself only as 'I am Brahman', and so it became the all.[8]

In the hymns of the Ṛig Veda Brahman had been a sacred word or hymn, the power of speech and magic formula. The origins and etymology of the word are still much disputed; some say it is from a root *bṛih*, meaning to grow or increase, and was used of sounds like the roar of an elephant. It came then to indicate power and strength, like the force or energy of the later Hindu term *śakti*. At any rate Brahman is a mysterious power, a holy potency, knowledge of which brings might and gives control over the universe. From there it was an easy transition to seeing in Brahman the primal power, the creative principle. But it is not merely a blind life-force, for 'it knew itself'.

As an all-pervading power the concept of Brahman (like the idea of *mana* and similar powers in other parts of the world) tended to bring everything under its sway. The effect of this unifying potency is seen in the merging of the soul with Brahman, and joining the gods into one. The seers are said to have known their union with the sun, and whoever knows that he is Brahman becomes all things, and the very self of the gods. The multiplicity of gods in the earlier pantheons is effectively dealt with in a series of questions. How many gods are there? The number is reduced from the original 3,306 to 303, then to 33, to 6, 3, 2, 1½, down to 1. For these gods are all manifestations of the one god who is the breath. He is Brahman, they call him that (*tyat*, the Yon).[9]

In a curious passage, which perhaps shows that this was a new idea or new application, the Vedic gods are said to have been ignorant of Brahman, and when it appeared before them they did not understand it. After a search among the gods only Umā, the beautiful daughter of the Himalayas, knew and declared that this is Brahman, the knowledge of which gives victory.

Brahman is discussed in various ways in the Upanishads and some of these show the influence of magical ideas. The classical Upanishads continue some of the earlier magical ideas, but instead of applying them to sacrifices as had been done previously, they fit them to the universe. We have seen that the many gods are reduced to one, which is Brahman as breath. Speech is also said to be Brahman, the eye is Brahman and so is the ear, and so the mind and the heart. These speculations appear materialistic, and especially so when Brahman is identified with food; yet all life depends on food, eating and drinking is the very process of existence. So the Taittirīya Upanishad says that Brahman is that from which beings are born, in which they live, and from which they depart. It is matter, life, mind, intelligence, bliss and food. He who knows this becomes immortal; he goes up and down the worlds, crying with joy: 'Oh wonderful, oh wonderful, oh wonderful, I am food, I am food, I am food . . . I who am food eat the eater of food, I have overcome the world.'[10]

This is strange to the non-Hindu, but it shows the pervasiveness of Brahman through all life and the identification of the enlightened knower with it; an idea that was to become dominant. More easily understandable is the identification of Brahman with space. Brahman is the space outside a man, and this is the same as the space within a man. The body is called the city of Brahman, and within the heart is a minute space, in which nevertheless heaven and earth are contained; this is immortal, sinless and real.[11]

If Brahman is infinitely small as well as infinitely great, then it transcends space and probably time as well. As the Upanishadic thought develops Brahman is no more identified with eating and breathing, but is seen as the origin and support of all life, indeed life itself. Brahman is the Imperishable (*avyaya*), eternal, all-pervading, present everywhere, the source of all creatures. As a spider puts out thread, and herbs arise on the earth, as hairs grow on the body, so from the Imperishable everything arises.[12]

The relationship of Brahman with the soul will be discussed in the next chapter. What is being said here is that the concept of Brahman led the Indian thinkers on beyond the old polytheism and mythology, to the idea of a world-ground and world-unity. In a progressive definition Brahman is said to be in sun, moon, lightning, ether, air, quarters of heaven, fire, water, mirror, echo, shadow, self and sleep. This is the secret meaning (*upanishad*). Brahman is the real of the real, the truth of truth (*satyasya satyam*).[13]

Finally the identity of Brahman with the universe is clearly brought out. Brahman is in front and Brahman behind, Brahman to right and left, Brahman below and above. Brahman is the whole universe.[14] The logical conclusion is pantheism: God is everything and everything is God. Or monism: only the one exists. This would seem to be fatal to religion, if man is left with no object of worship. But there might still be room for manœuvre in distinguishing between the real and the phenomenal, the spiritual and the material. This will be examined in the next chapter. Meanwhile, the strongly unifying tendency in Hindu thought affects all notions of creation.

Not inconsistent with the idea of unity, and perhaps a development from it, is the belief in the constant dissolution and recreation of the universe. This conception of creation is cyclic, ever rising and falling, but ever renewing itself like a circle, which is a type and symbol of eternity, 'of first, and last, and midst, and without end'. Really there is no origin of the world, since it is periodically destroyed and reborn. This doctrine is connected with the belief in the transmigration of souls, as will be seen later. But as far as the universe is concerned, its relationship with the divine is in being and becoming, flowing and reforming, in successive eons.

This seems to be a late idea, though perhaps inherited from the old culture which had been submerged by the Aryans invading India, but it does make its appearance in the later Upanishads. In the Lord (Īśāna) of all things, the whole universe comes together at the beginning and dissolves at the end. Or the supreme Brahman is unborn, he meditates on the world, awakens it into existence in thought, and dissolves it again into himself. Later it is said that at the end all existing things are burnt up, dissolved into the transcendent, beyond whom there is no existence nor non-existence. At the dissolution the whole universe is rolled up like a piece of cloth.[15]

Also in the later Upanishads is introduced the doctrine of *māyā*, which became a cardinal principle of Indian thought. *Māyā* in one sense is magic, deceit or fraud, and in another, illusion, unreality or supernatural power. Coming from a root *mā*, 'to measure or form', it meant the power of a god to change form, appear in a disguise, or produce illusions. *Māyā* is compared to the deceit of a juggler, or the illusion of a rope for a snake or mother-of-pearl for silver. So the gods are concealed by *māyā*, by appearances, manifesting themselves in many and changing shapes. By *māyā* the god Brahmā evolves the world, which has no existence apart from him, being imagined by him as a dream.

In the Upanishads *māyā* describes the 'illusion' that appearances are reality. It does not, however, deny the importance of appearances, but shows that they must not be taken as final reality. The sense of transitoriness, so important to Indian thought, is here. In the Śvetāśvatara Upanishad nature (*prakṛiti*) is said to be illusion (*māyā*), and the mighty Lord (*maheśvara*) is the illusion-maker (*māyin*). The whole world is pervaded with beings that are parts of him. And in the Bhagavad Gītā the creative power (*yogamāyā*) of the Lord veils him from the bewildered world, so that he reveals himself to whom he will. Through the Lord, imperishable and unborn, the mystery of his appearance in this world is brought about by his own power.[16]

The Bhagavad Gītā, the Song of the Lord, the manifested Kṛishṇa, is later than most of the classical Upanishads. But its authority is almost as great, and it expresses a personal religious faith which has made it the best known and loved Indian Scripture. The constant creations and dissolutions are indicated in the Gītā. The Lord pervades all the universe, he sends beings forth again and again, receives them into himself at the end of one cycle (*kalpa*), and then dispatches them again at the beginning of the next cycle, and so the world is ever revolving. The appearance and disappearance of the world is in periods of equal length, a day of Brahmā and a night of Brahmā (the personal creator as distinct from the neuter Brahman), each of which is a thousand ages long.[17]

In later myths and stories (Purāṇas) great fantasies were spun on to these beginnings. Brahmā was himself born from the navel of the supreme god Vishṇu, from whom all arose and into whom all returns. Indra, the chief warrior-god of the Ṛig Veda, was later presented as a divine king who lived seventy-one eons, and twenty-eight such Indra lives made up one day and night of Brahmā. Heinrich Zimmer, in his *Myths and Symbols in Indian Art and Civilization*, has retold in a charming way a story from the Purāṇas in which a small boy is sent to rebuke Indra's pride, telling him of many Indras before himself, Brahmās following Brahmās in endless series, and universes coming and going out of every pore in Vishṇu's body. While he is speaking a column of ants marches across the floor of Indra's palace. The boy stares at them and then laughs. Pressed by Indra to disclose his thoughts, he says that every ant was once a god Indra who had now become an ant again in the process of transmigration. Finally Indra is brought to humility and wisdom through the knowledge of his tiny role in the unending play of birth and death. In other myths the god Śiva, the lord of the dance (Naṭarāja, famous in art), dances in the play (*līlā*) of creation. But these are far post-upanishadic ideas.

Also after the Upanishads developed the popular Indian belief in cycles of universal existence divided into four ages (*yuga*). We are now in the fourth, the worst age, Kali Yuga, the dark age. This began on Friday, 18 February 3102 B.C. As a comparatively short age, owing to lack of the true doctrine, it will last only 432,000 years. But ten thousand times this period is only one day of Brahmā. Here so astronomical are the speculations that they lose all reality. But the principle is constant, that of the ever-moving process of creation and dissolution, the eternal ebb and flow, the merging of all into the divine and the real, and then the re-emergence of the phenomenal *māyā*.[18]

These theories are not found in the classical scriptures, though they are often quoted nowadays as typical contributions of India to world-thought. And modern astronomy, with the immense vistas of space and time that it has uncovered, light-years that might be taken as akin to *kalpas*, evolution and degeneration, makes Hindu speculations less strange to the West than they might have been a century or two ago. But whether in the Upanishads or later, the Indian world-views are all of them insistent, as distinct from much of modern science, on the primacy of the spirit. It is the One who enfolds all. All this is Brahman. To know this is to pass beyond the deceptive world of appearances (*māyā*) to the reality within and beyond all this.

'In the beginning God created.' 'In the beginning was the Logos.' So the two Christian testaments begin with statements about the origin of things. But Biblical thought differs from Indian ideas about beginnings and cyclic re-creations.

The Biblical accounts of creation are so well known that they are easily misunderstood. There are two distinct myths of creation in Genesis. The second in Genesis 2 is the older, coming from the J school of writers (who used the divine name Jehovah or Yahweh). Here the setting is the desert, with no rain or plants. Man is made first from the ground, an earthy man, though superior to all other creatures which he names. After the creation of man trees grow and the four rivers of the Near East rise from the ideal garden. Man is made from primary matter, as a doll from desert dust, and God blows into his nose to breathe a soul into him. The close connexion of soul and breath remains down the ages.

The first account of creation, in Genesis 1, is a late priestly, sophisticated and almost evolutionary story. Here man is made last, in the image of God, from above. The myth bears some traces of much older stories that were behind it, like the Babylonian creation myths. That light appeared before the sun has made the sceptic smile, but it is an echo of the Babylonian myth of the light conquering the darkness. Similarly the waste and darkness of the deep (*tehom*) recall the Babylonian flood deity Tiāmat. A world-egg, known in much ancient mythology as well as Indian, appears in neighbouring Phoenician story as produced by the wind. There is no egg in the Bible story, but the breath (spirit) of God broods on the waters; this word 'brood' occurs only twice in the Old Testament, and both times of a bird brooding. The emergence of dry land from the flooded plains, the water gathering together into one place, recalls the alluvial plains of Mesopotamia which emerge from the winter rains in the spring, and grass appears first; afterwards the sun's light becomes clear. The order of the creative acts may have the same background and the seven days of creation, such a trouble to the fundamentalist, may well have been the divisions in the story made to fit into daily readings at the seven days' celebration of the new year festival.

But while the Bible, like the Vedas, has a mythological background, as we have it now the first story of creation in Genesis is a highly edited priestly account. The Old Testament, indeed, is one of the most thoroughly edited of all books, and it underwent constant revisions and expurgations, in order to root out polytheistic and fertility suggestions. This reformation was of the greatest importance. Through it Christianity began with monotheism, purged from all polytheistic traits.

The priestly version of creation, made at a late period in Israel's history, is strongly monotheistic and influenced all later thought. In this story the anthropomorphic expressions, those that might suggest that God was in human form, are reduced to a minimum. God does not mould man out of clay here, nor does he walk in the garden in the cool of the day as in the J stories. 'In the beginning God created', and the word used here for 'create' (*bārā*) is used of God alone. Only God can truly create and man's power is essentially derivative.

God creates by his word alone. There is no taking a handful of dust or gouging out a rib. Later writers put it thus: 'by the word of the Lord the heavens were made . . . for he spoke, and it was done'. Speech is related to breath, and so the breath (*ruach*) of God brooding on the waste is connected with his creative word. In the great Psalm of Creation (104) it is said that when God takes away the breath (*ruach*) of men they die, and when he sends forth his breath again they are created and the earth is renewed.

In this same Psalm, and other writings, the wisdom (*hokmah*) of God is almost personified as the agent of creation. 'In wisdom hast thou made them all.' Proverbs, which sing the praise of Wisdom, see it as pre-existing creation. 'I was set up from everlasting, from the beginning, or ever the earth was. . . . When he established the heavens, I was there.' Wisdom is the active agent of creation: 'I was by him as a master workman, and I was daily his delight.'[19]

In the wisdom books of the Apocrypha this is developed further. Wisdom, speaking of herself, says, 'I came forth from the mouth of the Most High, and covered the earth as a mist.' In the creation of Adam, 'wisdom guarded to the end the first formed father of the world, that was created alone, and delivered him out of his own transgression'.[20]

So the divine Wisdom is glorified and personified. 'She is a breath of the power of God, and a clear effluence of the glory of the Almighty. . . . She is an effulgence from everlasting light, and an unspotted mirror of the working of God, and an image of his goodness. . . . She is fairer than the sun, and above all the constellations of the stars. . . . She reacheth from one end of the world to the other with full strength, and ordereth all things graciously.'[21]

In this wisdom teaching the unity of God is maintained, but the method of creation is said to be through wisdom, which is an effluence or power of God, but not a separate divine being. Thus in the godhead there is diversity in unity. The importance of this for Christian teaching can hardly be exaggerated.

In the New Testament the Logos, the word or reason of God, is the agent of creation. 'In the beginning was the Logos, the Logos was with God, the Logos was divine . . . all things were made through him, and without him was not anything made that was made.' In Colossians the divine Christ, the Son, is called 'the image of the invisible God, the firstborn of all creation' (or 'his is the primacy over all created things'.) And 'in him were all things created', both visible and invisible, 'he is before all things, and in him all things hold together'. In the epistle to the Hebrews the Son is called the 'effulgence' of God's glory, and 'the very image of his substance, and upholding all things by the word of his power'. These are profound teachings on the nature of the divine and the pattern of creating and sustaining the world.[22]

It is sometimes said that Indian writings are a biography of man. Whether this is so or not, and it has the fascination of a half-truth, it is clearly not true of the Bible. There are those who suggest that the older Christian belief was that man is the centre of all things, which revolve round him and his little world, and that this view is outmoded by modern science which shows this earth as a tiny dot (but not necessarily insignificant) in a vast cosmos. But such a view of man as central finds no support in the Bible, or in orthodox Christian doctrine. The world is created by God, and for the glory of God. Man is not the centre of the universe, in the Biblical view. There are other worlds, heavens above, and heavens of heavens, as well as waters below. Man is only one in the hierarchy of beings in this creation, and a fallen creature at that. His task is to glorify God, not himself: 'Fear God, and keep his commandments; for this is the whole duty of man.'[23]

God is 'all in all'. God is the supreme creator and controller, conscious and omniscient. The Bible never asks, as the Ṛig Vedic Song of Creation did, 'Who knows whence the world first came into being? He, the first origin of creation, he knows, or perhaps he knows it not.' Nor could the Bible say that in the beginning there was neither existence nor non-existence. But it would agree with the Chāndogya Upanishad, 'How could being be produced from non-being?' If the world was made from nothing (*ex nihilo*) it was made by God, and so not by nothing. God is eternal and uncreated, and his Christ is 'the first and the last and the living one'.

It is true that the Genesis story appears rather literal, and prosaic fundamentalists have tried to work out a precise date for the creation, like the Yugas of Hindu speculation. So 4004 B.C., on the 23rd October (after the autumn equinox) at nine in the morning, was calculated, and found its way into the margins of some older Bibles unfortunately. But the Bible itself has nothing of this in the text, and it often refers to its times and days as very different in the eyes of God. 'A thousand years in thy sight are but as yesterday when it is past, and as a watch in the night.' And again, 'As a drop of water from the sea, and a pebble from the sand; so are a few years in the day of eternity.'[24]

In creation the wisdom and purpose of God are never doubted. It is true that the plans of God are not always clear; how can man hope to fathom them? 'Where wast thou when I laid the foundations of the earth? . . . when the morning stars sang together and all the sons of God shouted for joy? . . . Declare if thou hast understanding.' But that there is a purpose in creation is never doubted, and this purpose is good, it is not mere play. 'God saw everything that he had made, and behold it was very good.'[25]

Hindu teaching is of a cyclic pattern, seeing a constant rise and fall, creation and destruction, birth, death and rebirth, of the universe and of men. Though it is true that the final aim of man is deliverance from the ceaseless round. But Hebrew thought rather favours a linear pattern, rising in a line from lowly beginnings, though with frequent falls, and so not inconsistent with later ideas of progress and evolution.

It is not so simple as that, however. There are variations in teaching. Ecclesiastes, perhaps the most unhebrew or pessimistic of Old Testament books, tends towards the cyclic view: 'one generation goes and another comes . . . all rivers run into the sea . . . that which has been is that which shall be'.[26] But this is unusual. The general teaching is that there are eons of past, present and future, and these depend on the will of God. There is no natural evolution or progress, as it were independently of God, for that would be impossible. There will be a better future, 'the day of the Lord', a Messianic age, a new heaven and a new earth. These things will be brought about by the sole will of God.

Yet though our times are in God's hand, human life is of great importance. Man lives in constant relationship to the righteous will of God. His progress or not depends on working together with God. And the very created world depends upon man's response to God. 'The created universe waits with eager expectation for God's sons to be revealed . . . because the universe itself is to be freed from the shackles of mortality and enter upon the liberty and splendour of the children of God.'[27] This Pauline saying reflects the whole Hebrew view of history and the revelation of God in it.

References

References are to the Upanishads and not to the Brāhmaṇas, unless otherwise stated, and so the word Upanishad will often be omitted.

A cheap selection of Hindu texts for the general reader is available in *Hindu Scriptures* by R. C. Zaehner (Everyman). Reliable and fuller translations are in A. A. Macdonell's *A Vedic Reader,* R. E. Hume's *The Thirteen Principal Upanishads* and S. Radhakrishnan's *The Principal Upanishads.* There are many English versions of the Bhagavad Gītā; those made by W. D. P. Hill and by F. Edgerton may be specially recommended. Quotations in this book are taken from these five works, by permission of the Oxford University Press and Messrs. Allen & Unwin, to whom acknowledgement and thanks are here made.

1. Chāndogya Upanishad 3, 19; Bṛihad- āraṇyaka 1, 2, 1; 1, 4, 1–17; Aitareya 1, 1.
2. Śvetāśvatara 1, 1 f.
3. Ṛig Veda 10, 81; 10, 121; 10, 72; 10, 90. Laws of Manu 1, 31.
4. Ṛig Veda 10, 129.
5. Śatapatha Brāhmaṇa 5, 3; Chāndogya Upanishad 6, 2, 2.
6. Īśa 8; Manu 1, 6 f.; Chānd. 3, 19; Śvet. 1, 1; 3, 4.
7. Kaṭha 4, 6; Ait. 1, 1 f.; Bṛih. 1, 4, 1–7.
8. Bṛih. 1, 4, 10.
9. ib. 3, 9.
10. ib. 4, 1 f.; Taittirīya 3, 10, 5.
11. Chānd. 3, 12; 8, 1–6.
12. Muṇḍaka 1, 1, 6–7.
13. Bṛih. 2, 1, 20.
14. Muṇḍ. 2, 2, 12.
15. Śvet. 4, 11; Māṇḍūkya 6; Subāla 2; Paiṅgala 1, 4.
16. Śvet. 4, 10; Bhagavad Gītā 7, 25; 4, 6.
17. Gītā 9, 7–9; 8, 16–17.
18. See Vishṇu Purāṇa, book 6.
19. Psalm 33, 6–9; Proverbs 8–9.
20. Ecclesiasticus 24, 3; Wisdom of Solomon 10, 1.
21. Wisdom 7, 25 ff.

22. John 1, 1 f.; Col. 1, 15 f.; Heb. 1, 3 f.
23. Ecclesiastes 12, 13.
24. Psalm 90, 4; Ecclus. 18, 10.
25. Job 38, 4 f.; Gen. 1, 31.
26. Eccles. 1, 4 f.
27. Romans 8, 19 f., in the *New English Bible*.

Chapter 3

THE ONE AND THE MANY

In the hymns of the Ṛig Veda the gods are exalted and mostly celestial, dwelling in the heavens: the sun, the dawn, the sky, the storm, the thunder. Indra, the most popular god of all, to whom a quarter of the hymns are dedicated, was the favourite of the Aryan peoples as they invaded India. He is both a thunder god and a warrior. Rushing like a bull he slays a primeval dragon, casts his thunderbolts, crushes his enemies, and drains the sacred soma drink in three great gulps.

The gods were the ideal of the Aryans and represented the virtues they admired. Like the Homeric deities, to whom they were akin, they fought in battle and boasted of their strength but never did a stroke of work. As Gilbert Murray said of the Olympian gods: 'They are conquering chieftains, royal buccaneers. They fight, and feast, and play, and make music; they drink deep, and roar with laughter at the lame smith who waits on them.... Do they promote agriculture? Do they practise trades and industries? Not a bit of it. Why should they do any honest work?'[1]

About 1500 B.C. the Aryan invaders came with their horses, recently domesticated, through the passes of the Himalayas down into the plains of the Indus river in north-west India-Pakistan. Here they found the ancient urban culture of those who, for want of a better word, we call the 'Indus people'. The latter lived in walled cities, with straight streets, central tanks and running water, and they had a form of writing that is still undeciphered. The illiterate Aryans overthrew these cities and despised their inhabitants, calling them black, snub-nosed, irreligious and unintelligible. This simply meant that they could not speak their language or fathom their religion. Indra's fighting perhaps represented the destruction of the Indus irrigation system, for we read in the Ṛig Veda that he broke down the fortresses, opened the cave where the floods were imprisoned, and set the seven rivers loose, while the black captives stood by watching under guard.[2]

For nearly a thousand years there are no traces of comparable cities to those of the conquered black Indus men, for the Aryans were nomads at first and only slowly settled down to mingle with the conquered, and impose their caste system founded upon conquest and colour (*varṇa*, the Sanskrit word for caste, means 'colour').

The Ṛig Vedic hymns depict the old ideas of many gods, and they have remained the most sacred of all Hindu verses, parts of which are still recited every day by millions of caste men. But the old polytheism was slowly modified. How far this was due to the underground Indus religion we do not know. Sir John Marshall said, 'Paradoxically it would appear that the Indus civilization transmitted to its successors a metaphysics that endured, whilst it failed utterly to transmit the physical civilization.'[3] But ideas are the most potent of all forces, and it is exceedingly hard to destroy a religion. The great gods of later and modern Hinduism give signs of having survived from ancient times; often they were fertility deities, concerned with agriculture and the family. Kṛishṇa and Kālī are both 'black' gods, and Śiva is Lord of Beasts as well as an ascetic yogi, and resembles closely a yogic figure surrounded by animals depicted on a seal found in the Indus culture ruins. These three are the most powerful gods of later and modern times. But already in the Upanishads Indra becomes a Brahmin student for 101 years, in the Gītā Indra's son Arjuna ('white') is taught by Kṛishṇa and in the Purāṇas Indra begs Krishna's pardon.

In the Upanishads the celestial and departmental gods are being merged into one, and as we saw in the last chapter the process of unification gathers in intensity till the 3,306 gods become one. The Vedic gods were all forms (*viśva-rūpa*), but now when people say 'sacrifice to this god or that', all is the creation of the one and he is all gods.[4] Brahman is the all-embracing principle, immanent in all beings. 'The one remains, the many change and pass.'

This monistic trend did not stop, of course, at the gods. It proceeded to embrace the soul as well. Truly the whole world is Brahman, from which one comes, without which one is dissolved. and in which one breathes. This is the self; smaller than the tiniest seed, greater than earth and heaven, including all works and all desires, this is my soul within the heart, this is Brahman.[5]

The word *ātman*, used for the soul or self, is believed to originate in a root *ān*, 'to breathe', and so would be the breath of life, the soul which animates man and gives him consciousness. But it is used in a great variety of ways and is often confusing to interpret. It means the ego or life monad, the immortal soul. It is also used of the lower or animal soul, and in addition as a reflexive pronoun for oneself. Moreover the *ātman* and the Brahman are continually used in alternation with one another, and it was clearly felt that the world soul is practically identical with the individual soul. The macrocosm is the same as the microcosm.

'In the beginning this world was Brahman', we have read. But also, 'In the beginning this world was the soul' (*ātman*), in the shape of a person. Then again, 'that great unborn soul, immortal, fearless, is Brahman. He who knows this becomes the fearless Brahman.' And again, Brahman was in the beginning, it became all, whoever knows it thus, I am Brahman, becomes this all.[6] Brahman is what western philosophy has called the Absolute, and to say that *ātman* is Brahman means that the individual soul is essentially identical with the Absolute.

This monistic teaching begins in the earliest Upanishad, the Bṛihad-āraṇyaka, and it is no wonder that in the following Chāndogya questions are asked in order to elucidate the mystery. Five great and learned householders undertook an investigation to discover, 'what is our soul and what is Brahman?' They consulted the sage Uddālaka Āruṇi, who led them to the knowledge of the universal soul.[7]

But the most striking answer to the problem, and the central text which became the most fundamental of all to Hinduism, occurs in the ensuing dialogues where the sage instructed his son Śvetaketu. The boy had been a student for twelve years, he knew all the Vedas and was very conceited. In nine illustrations the father revealed the unity of the individual and the universal. As salt dissolves in water and pervades it all, so that it can be sipped from any part, so does the world soul pervade everything. 'That is the real. That is the soul [*ātman*]. Thou art that.'[8]

This famous phrase, 'That thou art' (*tat tvam asi*), you are yourself that very thing, became characteristic of Hindu thought. It plainly means monism or non-dualism, though there were to be different interpretations of it.

This monism had been hinted at also in the teaching of the Inner Controller. The Inner Controller dwells in the earth, yet is other than the earth and the earth does not know it. It dwells in water, fire, air, ether, sky, sun, moon, space, dark, light, in all beings, in breath, speech, eye, skin, mind, understanding and seed, yet it is other than these. They are as spokes converging on him who is the hub of the wheel. Yet at the deepest level the Inner Controller is identical with the human soul, for the constantly repeated refrain is that while he dwells in all things yet is other than all things, 'He is your Self, the Inner Controller, the Immortal.' And later in the short, but thoroughly monistic Māṇḍūkya Upanishad, the Inner Controller is knower of all, source of all, beginning and end of beings, the entirely undifferentiated One.[9]

The Brahman is thus the Absolute. It is the sole existent, real and unconditional. All the world and nature is illusion (*māyā*) or play (*līlā*). Brahman is above and beneath, in front and behind, as is all this so is the soul above and beneath, in front and behind, and is all this. Both are indescribable, 'Not this, not that' (*neti, neti*).[10]

The great debate of the later commentators on the Upanishads arose between the complete monists or non-dualists, and those who sought some modifications of the extreme position. The non-dualist (*advaita*) school was most notably represented by Śaṅkara in the ninth century A.D. He taught that the soul is the same as Brahman, it is universal and infinite; it is existence, knowledge and bliss. A modified non-dualism was set out by Rāmānuja in the eleventh century A.D. who, while recognizing the unity of the soul and God, yet held that the soul is only one portion of the Infinite Being who is its Lord and far transcends it. And Madhva in the thirteenth century taught the complete subordination and dependence of the souls and the world on God; he even emended the Upanishadic phrase to read 'thou art not that' (*atat tvam asi*). These schools remain to this day, with the teaching of Rāmānuja invoked as support to the great popular cults, but the non-dualism of Śaṅkara held widely and often set out in the West as the chief Indian philosophy.

Logically complete monism or non-dualism would seem to spell the end of religion, for how can one worship oneself? Even the extreme Vedāntists seem to have felt this for they assumed the existence of illusion (*māyā*) or ignorance (*avidyā*), and while stating that reality is One without a second yet they accounted for the world by saying that it is illusion produced by Brahman, which suggests that there must be some duality within Brahman. And Śaṅkara himself often used the language of theism, and even composed hymns with the repeated refrain, Worship Kṛishṇa. But such worship was only regarded as a means of helping concentration and was inferior to pure knowledge. We shall see that the Bhagavad Gītā takes the opposite view.

In some of the Upanishads there is a tendency away from religious practice in the emphasis placed on knowledge. Reaction against the mechanically performed sacrifices and prayers of the priests was understandable and, like some of the Old Testament prophets about the same time, some of the Indian sages scorned sacrifice and compared the worship of household gods with that of dogs. The revulsion of the philosophers against popular cults, and the agnosticism of the Buddha and the Jains, must be understood against the background of the times. Even today there are blood sacrifices in places, and images everywhere. What must it have been like 2,500 years ago, in Benares and the Kālīghats?

In the main sacrifice was tolerated, but looked on as secondary.

Meditation could replace worship. So the Upanishads ask, Why sacrifice to this god or that? One should meditate on the soul alone as dear. Indeed the true sacrifice is the disciplined life of the student of sacred knowledge. Eventually this knowledge came to be regarded as superior to the scriptures themselves and to the disciplined life (*yoga*); not through rites but by hard study and attention to the teachers of Brahman do men attain salvation. And in the later Upanishads the conclusion is drawn that if the soul is lord of all, and is that which the Vedas praise, it does not need the Vedas. What use is Vedic study to him who has perceived the soul?[11]

If one is divine there is no submission to any superior spirit. There is no consciousness of I or Thou. One exalts and swells with might, realizing the soul as eternal, beyond space and time. 'Oh wonderful . . . I am food, I am deathless, I am Brahman.' This may be called mystical exaltation and union with all things, or manic egotism.[12] One should become almighty and all-knowing. And in fact many sages have claimed to possess the superior knowledge and divine life which remove them from all worldly cares. Great privations have been endured to attain *siddhis*, supernatural powers, visions and levitation. But the sceptic might say that such seers still do not possess all knowledge and they certainly do not escape death. The way taken by some of the Jain saints was to fast to death and so become completely free of *māyā*.

However, in the early Vedas, and appearing again in others of the later classical Upanishads, a worshipful relation of man to God is seen to be essential to religion. Even the earlier and basic Upanishadic passage, which had spoken of the universal soul as all things, had yet compared it to the hub of the wheel which held all gods, worlds and creatures together, and called it the Lord and king of all beings. Here at least the individual souls are dependent on the supreme, and while one with him they proceed from him.[13]

A beautiful picture is given in the Muṇḍaka and Śvetāśvatara Upanishads. Two birds, ever-united companions, cling on to the same tree. One eats the sweet fruit, while the other watches without eating. The first is the active individual soul, the other is the motionless universal Brahman. On the same tree a person grieves for his helplessness, but when he sees the other as the Lord (*Īś*) in his greatness, he is freed from sorrow.

Both the Śvetāśvatara and the Kaṭha Upanishads have strong theistic notes, though it may be questioned whether they consider that the supreme and the individual souls are really different. The Śvetāśvatara opens with a list of questions: Whence are we born? what is the cause? by what do we live? Not nature, chance, female or male persons can be the cause, or any combination of these, because of the existence of the soul. So it is the one Divine that rules over all things. He is the hub to which many spokes and parts are attached, and in his brahma-wheel the soul flutters about thinking that it is different from him. The aim of life is to know God and then chains fall off, sufferings are destroyed, and birth and rebirth cease. God appears both as immanent, he pervades all things, and also as standing opposite creatures. He is identified with Rudra, a deity of the Ṛig Veda (later to appear as the great god Śiva), the source of the gods and origin of the Golden Seed.

The Supreme One is now called Lord (Īś, Īśāna or Īśvara). He is all-pervading, dwelling in the heart of all beings. One and colourless himself, he gives colour and diversity to creatures. He is the wielder of *māyā* and acts through this power. The Absolute is without parts, but the God of worship has many forms. The wise seek the God who is the inner self of all beings; they go to him for refuge and find liberation in him.

In this Upanishad we get the nearest that these scriptures allow to a personal God, though he is an object of knowing contemplation rather than of worship; knowledge of him brings release and immortality. This is much nearer to theism than is the non-dualistic teaching. For the theist may well wonder whether in speaking of God, who by definition must be completely supreme, he is speaking about the same thing as the monist who, whether he refers to God or gods, regards them as ultimately illusory emanations from the undifferentiated Absolute.

But in the Bhagavad Gītā there is a great development which was to affect the whole course of Hindu religion down to this day. There is a revelation of the nature of God and a loving relationship to him.

The Bhagavad Gītā is a small book which emerges from the great Sanskrit epic the Mahābhārata. In it the god Kṛishṇa appears as charioteer to the warrior Arjuna, answers his questions and resolves his doubts by revealing to him the way of devotion. Kṛishṇa was very likely an ancient Indian non-Aryan divinity (his name means 'black'), and hence he was popular with the people. Now he appears as an *avatāra* (descent, 'incarnation') of the Vedic god Vishṇu. He is lord of all creatures, but he sends forth himself by the power of *māyā* into the world, whenever there is a decline of righteousness (*dharma*), to protect the good and destroy the wicked. The avatar doctrine is defended against critics who do not know that the revealed Lord has also a higher nature in which all things are sustained. He is the Lord (Īśvara) who abides in the heart of all beings.[14]

Clearly there is a religious advance here, though it is not always plain that there is a real distinction between God and the soul. Indeed the Gītā, for all its shortness, is very complex, and the word soul or self (*ātman*) is used in a variety of ways. At the beginning of the book the main concern is the soul, and Arjuna is assured that the soul is necessarily immortal and so cannot be defiled or destroyed by action. 'I, and thou, and these men, have always been and will always be.' Knowledge of the soul and its eternal nature, through the practice of yoga, brings realization of unity through Brahman.[15]

However, the most perfect yogi is then said to be the one who worships God full of faith. This is an entirely new note, and it is worked out in chapters 7–12. The Lord appears to be Brahman in personal form, and this would fit in with some former teaching; but the Gītā goes beyond this. Kṛishṇa reveals himself to Arjuna in a multiform transfiguration, and the astonished worshipper declares the supreme mystery that Kṛishṇa is true God: the imperishable, being and non-being, and what is beyond that, the primal person and the supreme abode.[16]

Moreover the revelation of Kṛishṇa is an act of grace, implored by Arjuna who when he sees the terrifying forms of God is overcome, but Kṛishṇa comforts him. That God could be affected by any feeling for creatures was strange to the Upanishads, for he is indifferent to and unmoved by them. This traditional view is slowly modified in the Gītā. The man who fixes his mind on God with devotion (*bhakti*) is 'dear to me', he who has renounced good and evil is 'dear to me', and those who follow by faith are 'dear to me'. And in the final chapter we read that the devotee is well beloved, and dear to God, and 'will come to me'.[17]

Rāmānuja, in his commentary on the Gītā, went even further and said that God loves the devotee beyond measure, cannot maintain himself without him because he is his very soul, and is unable to endure separation from him. This is both because God is an ocean of boundless compassion and also because, according to Rāmānuja, there is an essential difference between God and human souls. This difference makes possible the relationship of loving devotion.[18]

The Gītā does not go as far as this, but it does contain the ideas of grace and love, and shows that the proper attitude of man before God is worship and devotion. The devotee (*bhakta*) goes to God for refuge with all his being, and is fully devoted to him (as the Buddhist, in the refuge-formula, goes to the Buddha for refuge).

The way of worship (*bhakti-mārga*) is not the only path but it is held by the Gītā to be higher than the traditional path of the yogis who seek the Unmanifested by the yoga of knowledge. Kṛishṇa now says that the way of devotion is not only easier but better; those who worship him in faith and love are considered the most perfect in yoga.[19]

Later popular Hinduism gave great place to the many avatars of Vishṇu, especially Rāma and Kṛishṇa. In the Purāṇa tales the love-legends of Kṛishṇa are taken as symbolical of the love of God and man, and the great flowering of devotional (*bhakti*) verse developed the same theme. It might seem that the old Vedic polytheism had returned with Vishṇu, Śiva and Śakti, not to mention Gaṇeśa and Hanumān, the elephant and monkey gods, but underlying it all the unifying philosophy has continued and still asks, 'How many gods are there?' And as the Gītā itself says, 'there is no end to my divine manifestations'.[20]

Biblical theology also had to deal with the problems of polytheism and find a unitary concept. The patriarchs in Genesis seem to have had tribal and clan gods, El or Elohim (from the same root as Allah). Various names have survived the later revisers: El Elyon, El Roi, El Shaddai. We are specifically told that while God is the same he was known to the patriarchs as El Shaddai, and not as the mysterious YHWH (Yahweh, 'Jehovah') revealed to Moses.[21]

Other gods or spirits were revered, perhaps particularly by women, and the wives of both Jacob and David had household images which were large and solid enough to be sat on or put in the bed. Through the endeavour of priests and prophets to cleanse Hebrew worship of polytheism and idolatry can be seen many traces of other cults, bull worship, sacred poles, fertility cults and the like. At quite a late date Second Isaiah pours his scorn on those who cut down a tree to make an idol; with half they fashion the image and with the other half they make a fire to warm themselves.[22]

Whether Moses was a monotheist, believing in one God alone for all men, has long been disputed. He introduced Yahweh to the Israelites as the God to whom they were joined by a blood covenant, but although God's power was manifested in Egypt the Egyptians were not called to serve him. Certainly some of the later leaders thought that each nation had its gods. So Jephthah the judge told the Moabites to be content in the land that Chemosh their god had given them, while Israel was content with the land they had received from Yahweh.[23]

Monotheism slowly gained the upper hand, and it became fully explicit in Second Isaiah. Heathen gods are mocked as their idols are carted away before the invader: 'Bel boweth down, Beno stoopeth . . . They could not deliver the burden, but themselves are gone into captivity.' Those who trust in graven images shall be as blind and helpless as these works of their own hands. So in

Psalm 96 we read, 'All the gods of the nations are idols [things of nought], but the Lord made the heavens.'[24]

From the oneness of God followed his sole creating power: 'the everlasting God, the Lord, the Creator of the ends of the earth'. In his colossal hand all the oceans are gathered, with the span of his fingers heaven is measured, the great empires are but as the last drop of a bucket and the waste dust of the scales; he alone sits above the circle of the earth and men before him are like grasshoppers. This is anthropomorphic language, but it is used to show the inadequacy of all human categories to describe God; 'to whom then will you liken me, that I should be equal to him?'[25]

This is the dominant teaching of the Bible, its powerful and all-embracing monotheism, which fixed the course of development for Judaism, Christianity and Islam. Whatever traces there may remain of earlier beliefs, the Hebrew reformers made sure that the unity and majesty of God should be stamped on all the scriptures of the Bible. It has sometimes been suggested that this monotheism was an early development, a reflection of the patriarchal system of Genesis, with God as the all-Father. In fact, it seems to have grown up slowly, and to have flowered under the trials of warfare and captivity at a late date. It is a sophisticated attempt at presenting a unitary conception of the deity. The idea of God as father, while present at different stages of development, never shone as fully as in the later New Testament period, when the Jews were under the Romans and they and the Christians soon scattered abroad and their social system was broken up.

It might seem that this stress on the majesty and transcendence of God would leave little room for immanence. God was great, but far away. And the strong Hebrew emphasis on morality, the divine holiness and human sin, might appear to widen the gulf. Holiness meant separation, and God was separate from sinners and exalted far above them. 'As the heavens are higher than the earth, so are my ways higher than your ways.' Yet this same metaphor is used of the measureless mercy of God, 'as the heaven is high above the earth, so great is his mercy towards them that fear him'.[26]

The teaching of the unity and transcendence of God could also lead on to his nearness to man. 'I dwell in the high and holy place, with him also that is of a contrite and humble spirit.' The wheel goes full circle; for if all things are God's creation, and he alone has power, then he must contain and perform all. The same process took place in later Islam, where the utter mightiness of God bridged the gulf between God and man, as is expressed in the teaching of the union of God and man by some of the Ṣūfī mystics, notably by Abū Yazīd al-Bisṭāmī, al-Manṣūr al-Ḥallāj and Ibn al-'Arabī.

The immanence of God appears in the Bible, and although at one stage it was thought that his decree did not run in the underworld yet Amos denied this and declared, 'though they dig into Sheol [Hades], thence shall my hand take them'. A Psalmist less forcibly but more profoundly saw the presence of God everywhere: 'whither shall I flee from thy presence? . . . thou hast beset me behind and before, and laid thy hand upon me.'[27]

The concept of the Spirit of God reinforced the divine nearness, not only to the world but to and within man. The Spirit of God enters into man as the vital breath, in creation. The Spirit of God descended on men, to bestow upon them artistic gifts, or fill them with prophetic power. When the Spirit came upon Saul he was 'turned into another man' and God gave him another heart. And on the Messianic king the sevenfold Spirit of God would rest.[28]

We saw in the previous chapter that Wisdom was the divine agent in creation, and it is closely identified with the Spirit of God. 'She that is the artificer of all things taught me, even wisdom. . . . She pervadeth and penetrateth all things by reason of her pureness.'[29]

In the New Testament the Spirit of God comes upon the Messiah at his baptism, and upon the apostles at Pentecost. But God himself is Spirit, he is not only in temples and on mountains, but everywhere, and he demands that men should worship him in spirit. His presence is likened to the wind, and he that is born anew must be born of the Spirit, for 'that which is born of the flesh is flesh, and that which is born of the spirit is spirit'.[30]

The Messiah is also spiritually present with his disciples, and in the long farewell discourses in St. John's Gospel this is stressed again and again. The Spirit is 'another comforter', but it is also Christ himself. And the disciples are called to the most mystical union with Christ, wherein they are to 'abide in me, and I in you'. More will be said of this in a later chapter. Here it must be noted that this teaching is found in many parts of the New Testament, both in the Gospel where Christ abides in the church, or where two or three are gathered together, and also in St. Paul's teaching of the triumph of the Spirit over the law. Here in successive verses and phrases we read of 'the Spirit of God dwelling in you', 'the Spirit of Christ', and 'Christ in you'. He would be bold who would try to disentangle these efforts at expressing the ineffable into separate presences or persons.[31]

Through the Logos the transcendent God is present in the world, not only in creation but in the incarnation, and he remains perpetually with believers through the Spirit who mediates the divine presence to them. In this way the New Testament, in particular, tempers the teaching of God's transcendence. By the doctrine of the Spirit the immanence of God is clearly shown, though its implications have perhaps not been developed in later Christian teaching as they might have been. The presence of God in other traditions and different faiths, by the same Spirit, could be recognized today. St. Paul's words may be apt here: 'All these worketh one and the same Spirit, dividing to each one severally as he will.'[32]

But while the teaching of immanence may fairly be claimed from the Bible, it never reaches to pantheism. The Logos 'was in the world, and the world was made through him', but he is not the world. However much God manifested himself through nature, creating and sustaining all things, God is ever beyond and greater than nature. This is but one aspect, though a real one, of his might, and since God is infinite he can never be fully seen in the finite, nor ever identified with it.

In the same way the Bible, and later Christian teaching, never speaks of the identity of the soul and God. There is no trace of monism. Duality or plurality is assumed as essential to the maintenance of relationships within the Godhead (in the Trinity), and between God and man, in grace and worship. God is all-mighty, all-knowing, and all-holy. No man has any of these attributes. In this life man is constantly subject to sickness, error and imperfection. In the next life he may be fully sanctified by God, and united with him, but not completely identified with him. The importance of this consistent Biblical viewpoint for devotion and mysticism will be seen later.

References

1. *Five Stages of Greek Religion* (Oxford, 1925), pp. 67 f.
2. Ṛig Veda 1, 32.
3. *Mohenjo-daro and the Indus Civilization* (London, 1931), vol. i, p. vii.
4. Bṛihad-āraṇyaka Upanishad 1, 4, 6.
5. Chāndogya 3, 14.
6. Bṛih. 1, 4, 11; 4, 4, 25; 1, 4, 10.
7. Chānd. 5, 11 ff.
8. ib. 6, 1–16.
9. Bṛih. 3, 7; Māṇḍūkya 2 f.
10. Chānd. 7, 25; Bṛih. 2, 3, 6.
11. Bṛih. 1, 4, 8; Chānd. 8, 5; Subāla 5, 15; 9, 15; Paiṅgala 4, 9.
12. See R. C. Zaehner, *Mysticism, Sacred and Profane* (Oxford, 1957), p. 117, etc.
13. Bṛih. 2, 5, 15; Muṇḍ. 3, 1; Śvet. 4, 6 f, from Ṛig Veda 1, 164, 20.
14. Bhagavad Gītā 4, 6–8; 9, 11; 1, 8, 61.
15. ib. 2, 12.
16. ib. 11, 37 f.
17. ib. 12, 14 f.; 18, 64 f.
18. Quoted in R. C. Zaehner, *Hindu and Muslim Mysticism* (Athlone Press, 1960), pp. 189 ff.
19. Gītā 12, 2.
20. ib. 10, 40.
21. Genesis 14, 18; 16, 13; 17, 1; Exodus 6, 3; marginal renderings.
22. Genesis 31, 34; 1 Samuel 19, 13; Isaiah 44, 15 f.
23. Judges 11, 24.
24. Isaiah 46, 1 f.; Psalm 96, 5.
25. Isaiah 40, 12 ff.
26. Isaiah 55, 9; Psalm 103, 11.

27. Amos 9, 2; Psalm 139, 5–7.
28. Exodus 31, 2 f.; 1 Samuel 10, 6–9; Isaiah 11, 1.
29. Wisdom 7, 22–4.
30. John 4, 24; 3, 5 f.
31. John 15, 26, etc.; 15, 4; Romans 8, 9–11.
32. 1 Corinthians 12, 11.

Chapter 4

WHAT IS MAN?

Man, in the Hindu scriptures, is seen in the light of eternity. His mortal life is not the chief interest of philosophy; only as a manifestation or play of the divine is it important. *Māyā*, illusion or transience, applies as much to human life as to the visible universe. The body is perishable, we know, the reality is the soul which is eternal.

To the ascetic, illustrated in the story of an abdicated king, the body is a repulsive object: foul-smelling, unsubstantial, made up of bone, skin, muscle, marrow, flesh, semen, blood, mucus, tears, rheum, faeces, urine, wind, bile and phlegm, and afflicted with desire, anger, covetousness, delusion, fear, despondency, envy, loneliness, hunger, thirst, age, death, disease and sorrow. All this is perishing, so what is the good of life and the ever-revolving cycle of rebirth? The only hope for the soul is when it rises serenely up out of the body and appears in its true form in the highest light of the immortal Brahman.[1]

The body is compared to a city of eleven gates, which are the orifices. In the Bhagavad Gītā they are nine: two eyes, two nostrils, two ears, mouth, anus and organ of generation. The other two are the navel and the sagittal suture in the top of the skull through which the soul is thought to escape at death. The embodied soul dwells in this city, yet is unaffected by its actions, neither working nor causing to work.[2]

The seat of the breath and even of the sense organs is said to be the heart; the golden lotus of the heart is the home of Brahman and identified with him. In sleep the soul glides down thousands of veins and rests in the heart, and at death it passes out through them and goes to the rays of the sun.[3] The body is known to be produced by both parents, the seed is the self of the father, but the Upanishads are more interested in the process of birth as the channel of transmigration through which the soul passes in the course of its many lives, of which more will be said in the next chapter.

Breath is of great importance, and this was natural, for in many religions this invisible element is taken as representing the spiritual nature of man, which does not die when the body dies. Breath (*prāṇa*) gives life, and is the vital force, and when it is withdrawn life ceases. Breath is also spirit, as in the Bible, and from there it becomes the universal power within nature and a symbol for God. We saw that when the many gods were reduced to one that one being is called the breath, he is Brahman.

The analysis of the individual into his component parts was attempted many times and grew in complexity. It was most important to discover what was the essential being by which the ascetic could reach his goal, and even more what were the elements of the individual which survived into the next life. Various groups of organs of sense and action are suggested, and a popular one was that which distinguished five mortal parts and five immortal parts. The five mortal parts make up the material body, the five senses which are dissolved at death, whereas the five immortal parts survive. In early texts the immortal parts were often given as speech, breath, sight, hearing and mind. The later Sāṁkhya (enumeration) schools gave great care to elaboration of the categories of the material and mental principles in man. While the Buddhists analysed the individual into five components (*skandhas*) only, and declared that since all these disappeared at death there could be no immortal soul.[4]

In the Upanishads there is never any doubt of the soul and of immortality. The difficulty lies in determining the meaning of a number of terms that are used each of them in different ways at various periods of development. Each human being is a 'person' (*purusha*), and through birth is entangled in 'nature' (*prakṛiti*). The 'person' is often interpreted as a psyche or personality, though distinct from the mere ego (*ahaṁkāra*). But this term 'person' is also used sometimes of the supreme deity in a cosmic sense, and in the Gītā it is applied both to this and to the individual soul. The *jīva*, a word derived from a verb 'to live' (English 'quick'), appears as the animating principle, the vital breath, and is often also used of the individual embodied soul as distinguished from the universal soul. In Jainism the *jīva* concept is taken over and developed as the eternal soul. But in Hindu philosophy the *ātman* emerged (from a root sense of breath) as the foundation of the self, the universal self, active in everyone and fundamentally identical with Brahman and ultimate reality. It was this *ātman* that the Buddhists rejected, but unlike the Jains they did not replace it with a *jīva* of their own.

In the later Upanishads and the Gītā appears the conception of nature (*prakṛiti*) as compounded of three elements (*guṇas*, strands), and this was developed in the Sāṁkhya philosophy. 'The conscious person [*purusha*] abides within nature . . . he enjoys the food supplied by nature . . . and that which is to be enjoyed consists of the three qualities' (*guṇas*). And again, 'the self is characterized by the three qualities'.[5]

These three components of all existing beings are goodness, energy and dullness (*sattva*, *rajas*, *tamas*, variously translated, but with an ethical application in man). They are differently apportioned in various people, and where there is a predominance of goodness the person or soul is helped to its proper goal. The Gītā describes these qualities in some detail: goodness is pure and brings illumination and health; energy is of the nature of passion and arises from craving; dullness is born of ignorance and binds by negligence and sloth. But all these three are surpassed when the embodied soul is freed from birth and death and attains eternal bliss. Even goodness binds to action, and so when struggle ceases the soul passes beyond goodness. Even in this life, if completely detached, a man can get beyond good and evil, be the same to friends and foes, unperturbed by the qualities and apart from them.[6]

Upanishadic teaching is not materialistic, but spiritual or dualistic, and interest centres on the soul. Beyond the senses is the mind, and beyond the mind is the great soul. It is without form and eternal, and invisible to mortal eyes, though there are seers who can perceive it through their intelligence.

The life breath (*prāṇa*), the intelligent soul, enters into the bodily self to the tips of the hair and nails, as subtly and fully as a razor slips into a case. A popular image is that of the soul as lord of the chariot which is the body, with the intellect as the charioteer and mind as the reins. The senses are the horses (an image that Freud would have liked) and they range over many paths, but are brought under control by the good charioteer who has understanding and a restrained mind. Again, the soul is like a lonely swan who, when the body is asleep, looks down on the senses and moves away alone through this world and the next. It is the golden person (*purusha*) who dwells in the innermost but is free of the universe.[7]

Sleep had a fascination for the Upanishadic thinkers. It was akin to death ('Death and his brother Sleep'), and in its deepest undreaming levels might be identical with the state of the motionless mystic with his mind utterly emptied of all concepts. Simple observation showed that when the body is immobile, except for the animating breath, the mind or soul is awake. The experience of dreams taught them that, at one level, the soul could roam unhindered over vast distances, and meet people alive and dead. There are two states of a person, in this world and in the next. But in between is an intermediate state that links them; that is sleep, for then one can see the other states also.

On going to sleep the soul transcends the visible world and becomes self-illuminated. In a perceptive statement the dreaming soul is said to create its own world: there are no chariots or roads in the dream-world but the soul creates them by projecting them from itself: it projects roads, chariots and animals to yoke to them. It creates its own pleasures and delights, streams and lotus-pools, for the soul is a creator.[8]

In deep dreamless sleep, however, a person desires no desire and dreams no dream. As an eagle folds its wings and glides in stillness to be enfolded in its nest, or as a husband in the embrace of a beloved wife knows nothing within or without, so a person in the embrace of the intelligent soul knows nothing within or without. And so at death, creaking like a heavily loaded cart, the bodily self groans under the riding of the intelligent soul. As his powers fail the watchers say, 'He is becoming one, he does not see.' The soul departs, by the eye or the head, the life breath departs, he becomes one with intelligence.[9]

What is this soul that rides the body and seems most real in dreams? In a long dialogue an attempt is made to fathom the mystery. The god Prajāpati, the Lord of Creatures, once declared that the real self (*ātman*) is untouched by hunger, thirst, sorrow, evil or death, and should be the supreme object of study. Hearing this the great Vedic god Indra and the demon Virochana determined to discover what the self was. For thirty-two years they studied as Brahmin pupils under Prajāpati and eventually were told that the self is to be seen in the reflection in a pan of water. Virochana was delighted and went off to tell the other demons the identity of the self with the body and its pleasures. This hedonism is still the doctrine of demons. But Indra was dissatisfied, seeing that the body becomes blind, lame, crippled and dies; this cannot be the true self. So after thirty-two years' further study Prajāpati told him that the true self is the one that moves about in dreams. But even then Indra saw that the dream self suffers with the body and men weep in sleep. After thirty-two more years he was told that dreamless sleep is the true self. But he saw (as some others did not) that in dreamless sleep one does not even know of his existence; it is like annihilation. So after five more years, making a hundred and one in all, the final truth was revealed to the god Indra. The truth is that the body is mortal, but it is the ground or support of the bodiless, immortal self. That which is incarnate suffers pleasure and pain, but that which is bodiless is untouched by these. The supreme self is unattached but conscious; he who knows is the self and the mind is his divine eye.[10]

The oldest Upanishads, therefore, realized that the soul had a close connexion with the body, but also because of its deathless nature it was closely akin to, and ultimately identical with, the absolute Brahman. In waking life the soul is most separated from the Absolute through distractions or illusion. Fundamentally it should be completely unaffected by the doings of the body. Hence came the many attempts at ascetic and yogic discipline, to produce a constant spirit of withdrawal and indifference to the world. In sleep the soul is master of its own affairs, and in dreamless sleep it loses all knowledge of separation, but by its own nature the soul emerges again into the purest light of consciousness. In later Upanishads this final state (*turīya*) is a waking condition attained through yogic concentration, beyond the false knowledge of dreams and the lack of knowledge of the deep sleeper, to a state in which there is no slumber at all yet complete abstraction.[11]

The true nature of the soul was later held to consist of Being-Awareness-Bliss (*sat-chit-ānanda*, or *sacchidānanda*). This is hinted at in one of the early Upanishads where it is expressed as the nature of the supreme Brahman.[12] Since elsewhere man in dreamless sleep was held to enjoy pure bliss, above all pain and grief, so the equation of the soul and the Absolute was reinforced. Their real nature is beyond time and care: unconditioned being, unrestricted conscious thought, and unutterable bliss.

The world draws the soul down through ignorance (*avidyā*), but it also serves as a training ground for eternity. The world is illusory (*māyā*) and ever changing; but it can serve as a stimulus to emancipation from the cycle of transmigrations.

As transitory and painful the world and its ways are rejected; life in the world is unhappy, its pleasures are illusory, and ascetic withdrawal is the ideal. Yet there is a reality to be perceived through and behind the world. The Upanishadic view of the world need not be entirely pessimistic; for if the material is rejected it is because the spiritual is so highly prized. 'India rejects the *profane* cosmos, because it thirsts for a *sacred* world and a *sacred* mode of being.'[13]

The true end of man, according to the Bhagavad Gītā and the later devotional schools, is devotion to God. 'He who serves me with unfailing devotion, rises above the three *guṇas*, and is fit to become Brahman.' This goal is held out by the Gītā to all beings. For while use of the Vedas was restricted to men only, and to the three twice-born or upper castes alone among men, the way of devotion threw itself open to everybody. 'Those who take refuge in me, though they are lowly born, women, as well as men of the lowest caste [*śūdra*], they also attain to the highest goal.'[14]

In its views of man and the world the Bible is as divergent from the ideas of the Upanishads as it is in its doctrines of God. Indeed, the differences are perhaps deeper here. They show that two religiously possessed peoples can come to almost opposite conclusions on similar problems, because they have a radically different attitude to life.

It is commonly said that the Biblical view is life-affirming, while the Indian is life-denying. But perhaps it is not so simple as that. What is clear is that the Biblical religion is as materialistic as it is spiritual. In fact it does not separate body and soul distinctly, and the value and reality of the material world are never questioned. The world is the creation of God, which God contemplated after he had finished his work, 'and behold it was very good'.

The creation of man, we have seen, is as mythological in the Bible as in the Vedas, but there is no doubt that it is the work of God. Man is made 'in the image of God'. Whether this phrase implied the belief that God had a body or not is not certain, but the likeness of man to God is stressed. A creature, and dependent, man is yet 'but little lower than God', crowned with glory and honour, and with all other creatures under his rule.[15]

The Bible occasionally reflects the notions of many primitive peoples that death is unnatural and work bad. The stories of Genesis, at least, look back to a Golden Age when there was no death, no work and no clothes. The primeval couple were tempted into these things by a talking snake, the snake being a symbol of immortality as well as of sex (there is no mention of a Devil or Satan in Genesis, and Old Testament demonology is indefinite). But religiously evil is attributed to sin, to conscious disobedience to the known will of God.

Sin came into the world, according to Genesis, corrupting the goodness of creation; and this provided an explanation of the problem of evil, though not a complete one, as we shall see in a later chapter. But the world is still real, and in many senses good. The body is good, or can be so, and Christians were later urged to 'present their bodies' to God as a living sacrifice.

Celibacy is hardly known in the Bible. Some priests had two wives, and of the prophets Jeremiah alone, as far as we know, was told not to take a wife and that may not have been for his whole life. Marriage is constantly shown as the ideal; 'be fruitful and multiply' remains God's command to man. The later Christian monasticism and glorification of celibacy and perpetual virginity is foreign to the general spirit of the Bible, and no doubt is an intrusion from Manichee or even Buddhist sources, which brought in a conflict of matter and spirit that is unhebrew.

As a religion for this life, lived in the sorrows and joys of the family, and with work that was often regarded as inspired by the Spirit of God and done for the glory of God, the Bible set out a pattern that had a lasting attraction. So we read that the Spirit of God filled Bezalel 'in knowledge and in all manner of workmanship'. And there is a great hymn of praise of the various skills which come from God: 'He gave men skill that they might be glorified in his marvellous works.' Praise is given to the physician, the scribe, the ploughman, the artificer, the smith and the potter; for 'in the handiwork of their craft is their prayer'.[16]

The analysis of the nature of man, and the relationship of soul and body, are much less clearly considered. In place of the wealth of speculation in the Vedānta, with its fertility and ambiguity of terms, the Bible is limited and concerned with more practical problems of living and work.

There is no speculation about the composition of body and soul, about sleep, or about the eternity of the soul. God breathed into man, and he became a living soul (*nephesh*, like the Arabic *nafs*). And of all creatures it is said that they have the 'breath of life' in them.[17]

The union of body and soul was thought to be very close;

indeed so tightly were they entwined that the Hebrews had difficulty in conceiving of life of any worth without the body. At death the body perished, but the soul also seemed to contract and went to Sheol under the ground, where it led a miserable existence like a shadow. This led into considerable difficulties when the problems of a future life began to be faced more seriously. It is said that India saw the eternity of the self, while Israel sought the redemption of the body.

The word spirit (*ruach*), used of God in early books, came later to be used of man also, in the same way as the soul and apparently identical with it. So we read of 'the spirit within me', and God dwelling 'with him that is of a contrite and humble spirit'. There is also the profound saying that 'the spirit of man is the candle of the Lord'. But man is still a dependent creature, it is still God who 'forms the spirit of man within him'.[18]

In the New Testament both soul and spirit are used and appear to mean the same thing. Both words occur in the opening of the Magnificat, in simple Hebrew parallelism which repeats in the second line the thought of the first in other words: 'My soul doth magnify the Lord, and my spirit hath rejoiced in God my Saviour.'[19]

In Mark we read of serving God with heart, and soul, and mind, and strength (καρδία, ψυχή, διάνοια, ἰσχύς). This is the fullest analysis of self that can be found in the Bible, for generally it is not interested in such analysis of human nature.[20]

Consistent with the Hebrew acceptance of life as good are those parallels of the divine with the human which sometimes shock people of other traditions, but seem natural in the Biblical context. The anthropomorphic expressions used about God are made in full reverence, but with the feeling that God can best be understood by analogy from man who is his image and 'but little lower than God'. So God is spoken of as 'Our Father', not because of physical generation from him as in the old fertility cults with their divine families, but because fatherhood is the noblest human status. And God is asked to 'forgive us our debts, as we forgive our debtors', a request that the Muslim will not make because it suggests to him that God copies man. But Christ did not hesitate to say this, because it showed the important fact that we must forgive men their sins against us, if we expect God to forgive our offences against him.

The Hebrew view is not detachment from the world and its activities in order to gain salvation. Love to God and one's neighbour are parallel, and both compulsory. The world is real, even if it needs redemption, and man cannot say that he loves the unseen God if he does not love his visible brother. The heretical Samaritan fulfils the commands of God better by his compassion than do the priests who perform religious duties but have no charity.[21]

Man is a social creature, and the Bible recognizes this both in his life here on earth and in the goal held out before him. The kingdom of heaven is social as well as personal, and there is no isolation away from one's fellows, but rather incorporation into the company of the redeemed.

References

1. Maitri Upanishad 1, 3; 2, 2.
2. Kaṭha 2, 2; Bhagavad Gītā 5, 13.
3. Bṛihad-āraṇyaka 2, 1, 19.
4. E. H. Johnston, *Early Sāṁkhya* (London, 1937), pp. 16 f.
5. Maitri 6, 10; Śvetāśvatara 5, 7.
6. Gītā 14, 5 ff.
7. Kaushītaki 4, 20; Kaṭha 1, 3; Paiṅgala 4, 2; Bṛih. 4, 3, 11 f.
8. Bṛih. 4, 3, 10.
9. ib. 4, 3, 19; 4, 4, 2.
10. Chāndogya 8, 7 ff.
11. A. B. Keith, *The Religion and Philosophy of the Veda* (Harvard, 1925), p. 569.
12. Taittirīya 2, 5.
13. M. Eliade, *Yoga, Immortality and Freedom* (E.T., Routledge & Kegan Paul, 1958), p. 10.
14. Gītā 14, 26; 9, 32.
15. Psalm 8, 5–6.

16. Exodus 31, 3 f.; Ecclesiasticus 38, 6–34.
17. Genesis 7, 15.
18. Job 32, 18; Isaiah 57, 15; Proverbs 20, 27; Zech. 12, 1.
19. Luke 1, 46–7.
20. Mark 12, 30.
21. 1 John 4, 20; Luke 10, 30 ff.

Chapter 5

IMMORTALITY

Life after death is one of man's oldest and most persistent religious preoccupations. Among the earliest traces of men, in burials of the Old Stone Age, there are pots and dispositions of bones which suggest that these men believed in a continued existence after death.

Indian thought in classical times takes the immortality of the soul for granted. This is its most fundamental assumption. The soul is naturally immortal; it pre-existed and therefore will post-exist, for its inner nature cannot be touched by this changing world of *māyā*. 'The knowing self is not born, nor does it die. It has not come from anywhere, and has not become anyone [i.e. it is always the same]. Unborn, constant, eternal, primeval, this soul is not slain when the body is slain.'[1]

In a conversation, recorded twice in the earliest Upanishad, the sage Yājñavalkya teaches his favourite wife Maitreyī, who was a lover of Brahma-knowledge. To her question whether immortality could be gained through wealth, he replied that only through love of the soul can anything be regarded as dear, so that knowledge of the soul is alone worthy of effort. But this soul, like Brahman, is indescribable; it is not this, not that (*neti*, *neti*). It is unseizable, unattached, unbound, not injured, indestructible.[2]

The immortality of the soul is inherent in its relationship to God, for while Brahman is said to have existed in the beginning, one only without a second, yet the identity of Brahman and *ātman* conditions this. So we read, As thousands of similar sparks come from a fire, so manifold beings are produced from the

Imperishable and return there also. And in another verse it says, 'As sparks from a fire, so from this soul [*ātman*, as world-soul] all breaths, all worlds, all gods and all beings come forth.'[3]

In a person the name and the form (*nāma-rūpa*) are passing, but the living self is distinct. So the body dies but life (*jīva*) does not die. When the body gets thin, through old age or disease, then the person frees himself from his limbs and returns to the place that he came from. Like a great tree which continues to live, even though bleeding from blows to the branches and trunk, so does the body continue as long as it is pervaded by the soul. The true self dwells in the body as the city of Brahman; it is free from sin, and is not killed by the death of the body. These and many other examples illustrate the constant belief in the indestructibility of the soul.[4]

So in the Bhagavad Gītā, when Arjuna on the battlefield hesitates to fight his relatives, he is reassured by Kṛishṇa with a verse that occurs also in the Kaṭha Upanishad: 'If the slayer thinks that he slays, or if the slain thinks that he is slain, both of them do not understand; he neither slays nor is he slain. . . . He is not slain when the body is slain.'[5] This means that when the soul knows itself as eternal spirit (*ātman*), and not bound up with name and form, then it realizes its own true eternal nature and neither life nor death can touch it.

The next step was to consider the relationship of the immortal soul to the succession of bodies that it inhabits. The Gītā puts it thus, 'As a person discards worn-out clothes and puts on others that are new, even so does the embodied soul discard worn-out bodies and take on others that are new.'[6]

The idea of transmigration, or rebirth into different bodies (redeath as it was sometimes called), was to become fundamental to Hindu, Jain and Buddhist teaching. But it is quite absent from the early Vedic hymns, which go no further than wishing for long life for man, rather in the Old Testament manner, though here it is life among the gods. It seems likely that transmigration was an ancient belief of the aboriginal or Indus people, unknown to the invading Aryans and repressed for a while; but it was so powerful that it soon emerged again and conquered the whole of Hinduism.

This belief is found in many parts of the world, though it takes different forms. In India rebirth is believed to take place at many levels, human and animal, and it came to be associated with a moral judgement on the previous life. In Africa the purpose of rebirth is thought to be to ensure the continuity of the family, and so men are not reborn as animals but into their own family. In Europe the belief has had only a shaky career. Plato gave the best known illustration of it in the myth of Er son of Armenius at the end of the *Republic*, where souls chose their new lot before birth according to their previous actions and suffering and so with a moral significance.

The Sanskrit term *saṁsāra* means to walk or wander together or through, and so to go about, pass through a succession of states, and so birth and rebirth, transmigration, metempsychosis. It makes a hesitant appearance in the oldest Upanishads and applies to the universal circulation of all creatures. It seems quite clear that the Brahmins were ignorant of this teaching at first. Twice we read that both Śvetaketu, who had studied the Vedas for twelve years, and his father Gautama Āruṇi, were stumped by the questions of king Pravāhaṇa Jaibali: Do you know what place men go to from here? Do you know how they return again? Do you know how yonder world is never full? In all the worlds this teaching is said to belong to the royal or warrior caste only, the Brahmins never knew it and must learn the truth as pupils.[7]

Elsewhere the soul is said to be like a caterpillar which when it comes to the end of a blade of grass draws itself together, so does the soul draw itself together before entering another body. And as a goldsmith turns a piece of gold into a more beautiful shape, so does the soul make to itself a more beautiful shape like the gods.[8]

The progress of the soul when it leaves the body is variously described. The ascetic is said to pass into the light, to the world of gods, to the sun, to the Brahma-world, and not to return. But most people, including those who practise sacrifice and almsgiving, go to the world of the fathers, to space and to the moon. There they work out the residue of their works, and then return through air, mist and rain to become vegetable and food, and so are born through men and women again.[9]

It is here that the moral element comes in, which gives a new turn to the doctrine of transmigration. The future lot, both in heaven and again on earth, depends on previous conduct, on actions (*karma*). Those whose conduct here has been pleasant will quickly enter a pleasant womb (birth), the birth of a Brahmin, a Kshatriya (warrior) or a Vaiśya (merchant). But those whose conduct here has been stinking will enter a stinking womb, the birth of a dog, or a hog or a Chaṇḍāla (outcaste).[10]

The role of deeds (*karma*) in transmigration is given growing importance. According to its actions the embodied soul assumes various forms successively in different conditions. Mere sacrifice is said to be inferior *karma*, and if they have no other good works then those who have enjoyed the heavenly reward of sacrifice will enter this world again or a still lower one. But those who seek the knowledge of the soul, by austerity, chastity and harmlessness (*ahiṁsā*), they reach the Brahma-world, the stopping of rebirth, and so they do not return.[11]

There is apparently an intermediate stage, a temporary heaven in which the rewards of earthly action are, at least in part, worked out. The soul is not rewarded or punished by an immediate rebirth on earth, but before being transferred to another mortal body it experiences for a while reward or punishment out of the body. Enjoyment of the fruits of good deeds is to take place in a high heaven and, it is assumed, punishment for evil deeds is in some appropriate hell. After that rebirth, whether noble or base, takes place again on earth.

There seems to be an attempt here to link up with a popular early belief in heavenly rewards. This appears in the Ṛig Veda, and even more in the Atharva Veda, and the problem was to combine it with the doctrine of transmigration, with which it is hardly consistent. So there are Upanishadic texts which describe the journey of the disembodied soul to the moon, which is the door of heaven, and it stays there as long as there is a residue of good works, and then returns as man, animal or insect, according to its deeds and its knowledge. But it is hard to see what determining factors remain over, to decide the manner and place of rebirth. Therefore other texts say bluntly that after death the soul enters a womb again for embodiment, according to its deeds and thoughts.[12]

A further inconsistent idea, that is, ill-fitted to the notion of *karma* deciding rebirth, is the belief in a son inheriting the sins of the father. This idea is found in other parts of the world and would be natural enough in a simple system of inheritance, but not where the soul is held to pursue its own way, fundamentally in isolation. In one Upanishad we read that when a father is dying he calls his son, who lies upon him so as to receive all the father's powers. The father places in him his speech, vital breath, eye, ear, taste, and so on, and says, 'Let me place my deeds in you.'[13] This does not seem to have any moral meaning, for no destiny is fixed by it, but it does agree with other passages which show the father being born again in the son, and this is strictly inconsistent with the view of the soul transmigrating and being born to a higher or lower estate according to its actions.

Quite how the deeds which determine rebirth affect or are attached to the soul is not clear. They seem to cling to it as defilement or blessing; but then again the true self is often said to be unaffected by the antics of the body. When the Sāṁkhya teaching thought nature to be made up of three elements (*guṇas*) of goodness, energy and dullness ethically in man, then the kind of existence to which the individual would transmigrate was thought to depend on the proportions of the three within him. Hence effort should be directed to increasing and ensuring the dominance of goodness. But finally one should pass beyond the range of these elements to attain complete salvation or isolation (*kaivalya*).[14]

The question of the memory of previous lives is not clear either. Those in the West who are unfamiliar with or sceptical about transmigration often make this a point of proof. If we could recall our previous experiences, then that might provide evidence for them. But, in the Upanishads, belief in transmigration does not depend on arguments from memory. It is based on the conviction of the indestructibility of the soul, though no doubt memory of other lives might reinforce faith in their continuity.

That the soul after death could recall its past existence might seem evidence of the continuation of a real personality from one life to the next; though the Buddhists have denied this while they still maintain the idea of the round of births and rebirths. In some of the later Upanishads it is said that the unborn child in the womb still remembers its previous life, but the pains of birth can deprive it of this memory. All that one can trace in the earlier Upanishads is the belief that according to the purpose one has in this world so does he become on leaving here, and by whatever one is thinking so does one enter into life. And in the Bhagavad Gītā great importance is attached to right thoughts at the moment of death; of whatever state of being a man thinks as he gives up his body, so to that being he attains.[15]

But of accounts of memories of previous lives, the classical scriptures have nothing. It was left to the much later stories, both Hindu and Buddhist, to relate in lavish detail the many previous lives of great men and gods, and by implication of ordinary mortals also.

Belief in the round of *saṁsāra*, the wheel of existence in which all men are caught up, a cycle that goes on endlessly with souls rising and falling in the scale again and again, this led to a view of the vanity of mortal life which could easily become pessimism, if there was no way out of transmigration. All is perishing: mosquitoes, grass, trees, warriors, world rulers, demons, ghosts, oceans, mountains, the pole star, and the very gods themselves. In this cycle of existence (*saṁsāra*) what is the good of the enjoyment of desires, when after a man has fed on them he returns repeatedly to this world? In this round of existence man is like a frog in a waterless well; how can he escape?

The Maitri Upanishad deals with these questions at some length. The answer given is that the true self is unaffected by the fruits of action; it is pure, unstained, and free from desire, and it remains detached like a spectator from the deeds of the body. Those who are attached to earth, or even to a son, wife or family, cannot attain to such independence. But the perfected yogi looks down on the wheel of births and deaths, as a charioteer looks down at the revolving wheel of his chariot. Even the mind which seeks the truth has to be cleansed and perfected by effort, for thoughts as well as actions can bind to transmigration. One's own thought is *saṁsāra*, and what a man thinks that he becomes. So by the serenity of thought one should destroy all actions, good and bad, that bind to this life. If the mind is fixed on Brahman it will become free from bondage.[16]

The round of transmigration seems to work automatically and carry with it all men and gods. But in the more theistic Śvetāśvatara Upanishad God is declared to be the motive and disposer of all. He is the inner self of all beings, the ordainer of all deeds, the author of time, and cause of earthly existence (*saṁsāra*), and of both continuance in bondage and of liberation (*moksha*).[17]

The Biblical view of the soul and its fate differs from the Indian because of variant presuppositions. There is, on the one hand, the Hebrew stress on the transcendence of God and the dependence of man, contrasting with the Indian view of the similarity and mutual absorption of Brahman and the soul. On the other hand, there was the unified view of the human personality in Hebrew thought, which could hardly consider soul and body independently of one another.

Old Testament ideas about the soul, its origins and destiny, are vague and confusing; and its views on life after death are so inadequate as to constitute the great weakness of ancient Hebrew (but not New Testament) teaching, compared with the Hindu profusion of beliefs in the beyond and certainty of the indestructibility of the soul.

In the older creation story the body of man came from the dust, and the breath of man from the breath of God. And later in the same story we read, 'dust thou art, and to dust shalt thou return'. But in the later book of Ecclesiastes it is said that the dust returns to the earth as it was, and the spirit returns to God who gave it.[18]

Genesis has the vague suggestion that man might have lived for ever, if he had not eaten of the tree of knowledge. Like many ancient peoples the Hebrews seem to have thought that death, like work and clothing, was unnatural. Later moralists ascribed death to sin, and St. Paul reflected the current Jewish idea that 'through one man sin entered into the world, and death through sin'. A modern theologian supports this, and gibes at 'the sentimental notion that death is "natural", a necessary and beneficial aspect of the ordering of nature'.[19] It may be questioned how many other Christians would now agree with this. What else is death but natural? There is little enough in the Bible about this, and the fact of death is accepted generally without argument.

Of life independent of God the Bible knows nothing. So there is no natural immortality, in the atheistic Jain or Sāṁkhya sense. This would have implied pre-existence as well as post-existence, and little is said in the Old Testament about either. It is generally assumed that the Jews thought the soul to be created at or before birth, and each soul independently of others, to live its own span of threescore years and ten. But in fact all that is said is that God breathed into man the breath of life and man became a living soul.

The Biblical emphasis is constantly on the creating power of God, and this overshadows speculation about the nature of man. 'So obsessed', says R. C. Zaehner, 'do the Jews appear to have been with the Majesty of God and man's utter insignificance that they forgot that man became a "living soul" by the fact that God breathed into him the "breath of life", the Holy Spirit, which is by definition immortal.'[20]

Hence the pre-existence of the soul in God would not be inconsistent with Biblical teaching, but a natural deduction from it, though it hardly ever becomes explicit. Later Christian scholastics and mystics were to develop the idea of the eternity of the human soul as an eternal idea dwelling in God, for in the divine wisdom are models or forms of all things, and while they are different in their relations they are not really distinct from the divine essence.[21]

In the New Testament period there are some slight suggestions of new beliefs impinging upon the Hebrew. There is the disciples' question about the man born blind, 'who sinned, this man or his parents, that he should be born blind?' The only possible answer seems to be something on the lines of *karma* and rebirth, and a modern commentator says that this 'implies a doctrine of pre-existence' which is a 'Greek rather than a Jewish idea'. Similarly the Jewish historian Josephus gave the surprising opinion that the 'Pharisees hold that every soul is imperishable, but that the souls of the good alone go to another body, while those of the wicked are punished with everlasting vengeance.' Josephus adds his own view that 'pure and obedient souls obtain a most holy place in heaven, from whence in the revolution of the ages they are sent again into pure bodies'.[22] It must be remembered that this was written during the full flood of Greek influence upon Jewish thought. If Josephus is correct there would seem to be some inconsistency with the doctrine of the resurrection, in which the Pharisees are also said to have believed. In any case Josephus is non-biblical, though contemporary with some of the New Testament.

The occasional references to a 'return of Elijah' (still allowed for in the Jewish Passover), which are sometimes quoted in support of a belief in rebirth, do not really mean this. 'The only escape' from death which ancient Hebrew belief allowed 'was ascension alive into heaven—as in the singular instances of Enoch and Elijah' and, it may be added, Moses.[23] But since these prophets were believed not to have died, so they would not need to be reborn as children, but would descend from heaven in power. The New Testament, it is known, interpreted the return of Elijah as a coming in spirit, in the person of John the Baptist.

Life after death, to the ancient Hebrews, was a dark and unhappy affair. Believed in by the people, in common with most contemporary nations, 'the realm of the dead, the rites connected with death and burial, as well as the destiny of the soul in the other world, play no part in the religion of YHWH. This is one of the most astonishing features of Israelite religion. That the spirit of the deceased lives on apart from the body is the belief of the people, but Biblical faith draws no religious or moral inferences from this notion.'[24]

Archaeological excavation has shown, in Palestine and elsewhere, that great care was given to graves, and the tools and weapons placed there testify to the belief that the departed spirit would need to use them. Some tombs remained sacred places down the ages; the graves of Sarah and Deborah, the sanctuaries of Shechem and Kadesh, for example, were hallowed by association with the ancestors and long remained holy places, some of them even to this day.

The dead were believed to go underground, since they were buried in the ground. Cremation was not practised as it was in India. Underground was a dark world of shades, Sheol, like the Greek Hades. It was a place of darkness, cold, forgetfulness, and a land of no return. It was from the subterranean world that the medium of En-dor raised up Samuel's ghost to speak with Saul. Psalm 88 gives a vivid picture of the land of forgetfulness, where the shades (*rephaim*) dwell in the dark and do not praise God.

Here was one of the most shocking features of Old Testament belief, that makes some of the Psalms 'improper on the lips of a Christian congregation'. For it is said bluntly that 'in death there is no remembrance' of God, 'shall they that are deceased arise and praise thee?' Because death was impure and in a dark forgotten place, so the divine decree did not run there. There was no judgement, no reward or punishment, no fruits of *karma* or hopes of heaven, for the dwellers in Sheol.[25]

Occasionally a prophet felt that God must be able to do something even in that shadowy place. 'Though they dig into Sheol, thence shall my hand take them', said Amos. And later a Psalmist said even better, 'if I make my bed in Sheol, thou art there'. But generally the most that could be hoped for was long life, on this sunlit earth; 'and I shall dwell in the house of the Lord for length of days'.[26]

It was not that belief in some kind of existence after death was lacking, but that the Hebrews, and in particular the prophetic and priestly editors of the Old Testament, could not see beyond Sheol. Concerned to abolish pagan cults of the dead and spiritualistic seances, they stressed the majesty of God: 'And when they shall say unto you, Seek unto them that have familiar spirits and unto the wizards, that chirp and mutter: should not a people seek unto their God?'[27]

Furthermore, the belief in the close connexion of soul and body made it hard for the Hebrews to conceive of any further active existence after the death of the body. When the idea of the resurrection of the dead does finally appear, right at the end of the Old Testament, then the bodies are raised up too, apparently to a further earthly existence. In a late passage in Isaiah there is hope that 'thy dead shall live; my dead bodies shall arise . . . and the earth shall cast forth the dead'. But it is questionable whether this refers to a resurrection of the dead or to a national revival. Only after the persecution of the Maccabees had forced men to think about the lot of the righteous dead, and perhaps under the pressure of Zoròastrian thought with its strong conviction of a future judgement and heaven, does belief in a resurrection appear. This could still be life on earth however: 'Many of them that sleep in the dust of the earth shall awake, some to everlasting life, and some to shame and everlasting contempt.'[28]

With the emergence of belief in a resurrection the Bible, or rather the New Testament, at last produced a doctrine worthy of comparison with beliefs of other religions, though still needing careful exposition. 'The belief in resurrection, in judgment, and retribution in the afterlife gradually came into being. The soul found a way to God after death. This doctrine remedied what was a serious defect in the early religion compared with paganism.'[29]

To turn to the New Testament is to enter another world, of light and hope. Faith in 'Jesus and the resurrection' was the main article of Christian belief. This is everywhere in the epistles, after the resurrection of Christ, but it also conditions the Gospels which were written after the event though recording the history before it.

Debate over the resurrection of the dead was active among the Jews in New Testament times. The Pharisees, who represented the great body of the Jews, held to it. The Sadducees who were the priestly and wealthy class rejected it because, they said, it was not taught in the Torah, the first five books of the Old Testament and core of the sacred revelation. Hence in his only debate with them Jesus quoted from Exodus to support faith in life after death: 'I am the God of Abraham', spoken to Moses, meant that Abraham was still alive. God 'is not the God of the dead, but of the living'.[30]

With faith in the resurrection of Christ as their main argument for a general resurrection, the nature of the body raised presented a problem to Christians. The resurrection of the flesh, the gathering together of the material elements to be conjoined to the soul, has been taught by many Christians and Muslims, who for this reason have rejected cremation. On the other hand the notion of a resuscitated body is thought to be not only impossible but repugnant by Hindus and Buddhists and by many modern Christians.

But St. Paul in his letter to the Corinthians tried hard to discriminate between flesh and spirit, and to show that resurrection is not mere resuscitation. 'But some one will say, How are the dead raised? and with what manner of body to they come? . . . Thou sowest not the body that shall be, but a bare grain . . . but God gives it a body even as it pleased him.' The happy choice of illustration from the grain that is planted and the living shoot that emerges led Paul to say, 'It is sown a natural body, and it is raised a spiritual body . . . and this corruptible must put on incorruption, and this mortal must put on immortality.'[31]

It might be objected that to speak of a body for a spirit is contradictory, or nonsensical. But some kind of symbol must be used lest we lose ourselves in vagueness. What this teaching tries to secure is the continuation of personal identity. This would seem to be essential if there are to be relationships between the soul and God.

St. Paul clearly does not teach the resurrection of the flesh. 'What Paul means is not that there is to be a restoration of the fleshly particles of the deceased, but that each individual will have bestowed upon him, as God sees fit, a spiritual body, that is, a body of another order than flesh and blood.'[32]

There are important consequences of this belief, if they are applied to the resurrection of Christ, after whose model the Christian is said to be raised up. And Christian emphasis on the resurrection of Christ also determined the certainty of belief in individual immortality. So that from its feeble beginnings, the Bible ends with the most positive and highly symbolical view of life after death, described in the book of Revelation. The nature of that world and final bliss is the subject of the next chapter.

References

1. Kaṭha Upanishad 2, 18.
2. Bṛihad-āraṇyaka 2, 4; 4, 5.
3. ib. 2, 1, 20; Muṇḍaka 2, 1.
4. Bṛih. 4, 3, 36; Chāndogya 6, 11.
5. Bhagavad Gītā 2, 19.
6. ib. 2, 22.
7. Bṛih. 6, 2; Chānd. 5, 3.
8. Bṛih. 4, 4, 3.
9. ib. 6, 2, 15 f.
10. Chānd. 5, 10, 7.
11. Śvetāśvatara 5, 11; Muṇḍaka 1, 2, 10; Chānd. 8, 15; Praśna 1, 10.
12. Kaṭha 5, 7.
13. Kaushītaki 2, 15.
14. E. H. Johnston, *Early Sāṁkyha*, pp. 34 ff.
15. Garbha Upanishad 3, 4; Chānd. 3, 14, 1; Praśna 3, 10; Gītā 8, 6.
16. Maitri 1, 4; 2, 7; 6, 28; 6, 34.
17. Śvetāśvatara 6, 16.
18. Genesis 3, 19; Ecclesiastes 12, 7.
19. A. Richardson, *A Theological Word Book of the Bible* (S.C.M., 1950), p. 60.
20. *At Sundry Times*, p. 177.
21. *Mysticism, Sacred and Profane*, p. 189.
22. G. H. C. Macgregor, *The Gospel of John* (Hodder & Stoughton, 1928), p. 225. Josephus, *Antiquities*, xviii, 1, 3; *Wars of the Jews*, 3, viii, 5.
23. Y. Kaufmann, *The Religion of Israel* (E.T., Allen & Unwin, 1961), p. 316.
24. ib. p. 311.
25. Psalm, 6, 5; 88, 10.
26. Amos 9, 2; Psalm 139, 8; Psalm 23, 6 (R.V. margin).
27. Isaiah 8, 19.
28. Isaiah 26, 19; Daniel 12, 2.
29. Kaufmann, op. cit., p. 431.
30. Mark 12, 27.
31. 1 Corinthians 15, 35 ff.
32. Richardson, op. cit., p. 35.

Chapter 6

HEAVEN AND BLISS

The nature of existence immediately after death, whether in heaven or hell, long engaged Indian attention. Many ideas were current in popular belief about the celestial regions, and although they might seem inconsistent with belief in transmigration or ultimate liberation, yet some theologians in later Vedāntic philosophy were not averse to reintroducing descriptions of Paradise.

While the earliest Upanishads were content with references to the soul going to the moon and the world of the fathers, the Kaushītaki Upanishad gives more particulars. Those who leave this world go to the moon, which is the door of heaven. There the soul is tested. Those who fail return to the world as insect, animal or man. But he who answers properly proceeds further. First he comes to the world of the gods, and finally to the world of Brahmā. The Brahma-world is depicted in some detail: in it there are lakes, rivers, trees, cities, thrones, couches, flowers and nymphs. 'Five hundred nymphs [*apsarasas*] go towards him, with fruits, ointments, garlands, garments and perfumes in their hands; they adorn him with the adornment worthy of Brahmā.' He comes to a lake and crosses it with his mind, he comes to the moments and they flee from him, he comes to the ageless river and crosses it with his mind alone. There he shakes off his good deeds and his evil deeds. He is now untouched by good and evil deeds, and all pairs of opposites, like a charioteer who looks at the revolving wheels but is untouched by them. So devoid of good and evil, the knower of Brahman goes on to very Brahman.[1]

Later popular Purāṇas went into great detail about the various heavens, of Indra, Śiva, Vishṇu and Brahmā. They were in the Himalayas, or thousands of miles above the earth, with all kinds of pleasures and delights. There were also the many hells, icy cold as well as hot, stocked with well-fed demons, and presided over by Yama, originally the first man to die and later god of the dead and the underworld.

In the Kaṭha Upanishad there is an ancient story of a descent into the underworld. The boy Nachiketas is sacrificed by his father and goes to the abode of Death (Yama). He waits for three days without food, and as recompense Yama offers him three gifts or wishes. Nachiketas's first wish is that his father may be appeased and receive him graciously on return to the earth. This is granted, as is also the second inquiry about the dwellers in heaven; Death tells him how to set up the proper sacrificial fire that leads to heaven. But the third question is the major one: when a man is dead, some say he exists and others say he does not. What is the truth of it? Death tries to avoid this question; even the ancient gods were not sure of it, so do not press me now, choose another boon, and do not ask about death. But Nachiketas presses his point: what is there in the great passing-on? And finally Death reveals the secret: 'The knowing self is never born and does not die at any time. . . . It is unborn, eternal, abiding and primeval. It is not slain when the body is slain.' This is the truth of the indestructible *ātman* which we heard of before. The same answer is given in the Bhagavad Gītā, to allay the scruples of Arjuna on the battlefield.[2]

In other texts the passage from this world to the next is sometimes compared to a bridge, as it was in Persian theology. The soul is the bridge, the separating boundary for keeping these worlds apart. Age and death do not cross over that bridge, nor well- or ill-doing; all evils turn back because the Brahma-world is free of evil. Whoever crosses that bridge is enlightened and wounds and afflictions leave him. But the only ones who find the Brahma-world are students of sacred knowledge.[3]

Elsewhere we read that the Brahma-world is won by good deeds; and again that ascetics through knowledge and renunciation attain the Brahma-world and are liberated. The perfect soul obtains the uncreated world.[4]

The Taittirīya Upanishad gives the song of triumph of him who on departing this world and reaching that self which consists of bliss, goes up and down those worlds, eating what food he desires, assuming what form he wishes, and singing the chant, 'Oh wonderful . . . I have overcome the whole world. I am brilliant like the sun.'[5]

The early Chāndogya Upanishad says that the Brahma-world is entered every day in deep sleep, but not fully attained. Just as men walk over treasure hidden in a field, so do all creatures go day after day into the Brahma-world, and yet they do not find it, for they are led astray by untruth.[6]

At death, however, unification with the divine slowly takes place. The watchers by the bedside of a dying man say, 'He is becoming one, he does not see', smell, taste, and so on. The point of his heart is lit up and by its light the soul leaves through the eye, the head, or another bodily aperture; he becomes one with intelligence. The different parts of the body and the organs all go, perfected souls enter into the All; dwelling in the Brahma-worlds, they are liberated at the end of time beyond death.[7]

This brings us to the question that we have touched on earlier. What is the final goal, beyond the round of birth and death? When all *karma* is worked out and the soul is perfected, with nothing left to draw it back to earth, what is its final destiny?

The great preoccupation of Hindu thought was 'liberation' from this phenomenal world, and from return to it. The word used is *moksha*, salvation or liberation or liberty. This comes from a root (*much*) meaning to set free, to release, to deliver; so *moksha* is the final emancipation of the soul. Various other aims of human life are recognized, which may justifiably take up a good deal of one's time in the world, in youth and in the mature life of the householder; such are material possessions, pleasure and duty. But *moksha* is the final human good, the ultimate aim, to which all should come in the end, and the only way of avoiding rebirth into another worldly life.

The Maitri Upanishad says that self-conceit binds one to the stream of qualities, and on achieving the opposite of this one is liberated. So, to be free from determination, free from self-conceit, this is the pathway to Brahman here in this world, this is the mark of liberation (*moksha*).[8]

The Praśna Upanishad sees the ordinary mortal rising to the moon and then returning again to the earth. But he who has meditated on the highest person, with the especial aid of the mystic syllable AUM, becomes freed from his sins as a snake is freed of its skin; he goes to the Brahma-world and has the vision of the supreme Person. And the Muṇḍaka Upanishad says that purified ascetics dwell in the world of Brahmā and at the end of time are all liberated and one with the immortal.[9]

The more theistic Śvetāśvatara Upanishad says that God is the cause of transmigration and of liberation. 'To that God do I, desirous of liberation, go for refuge.' Similarly in the Gītā, he who knows the uncreated God is himself undeluded and freed from all sins. In his commentary on this passage Rāmānuja later was to differentiate between God and the liberated soul: 'the Lord is different in kind from the liberated soul which, though unborn, nonetheless has a beginning, for the "unborn" condition of the liberated soul has a beginning.'[10]

Another word used of the final goal is cessation, separation, completion or tranquillity (*nirvṛitti*). 'This indeed is the way. This is immortality. This is complete union and peacefulness' (*nirvṛitatva*). As a spider climbing a thread obtains freedom, so does one who meditates thus.[11]

This joins up with *nirvāṇa*, a word that is chiefly Buddhist and Jain, though not exclusively so. Not found in the older Brahminical texts, *nirvāṇa* appears in the Gītā and later Hindu writings and is commonly used today. The word is illustrated by the metaphor of a flame which is blown out. *Nir-vā* (*vā*, as wind, plus *nis*) is to be blown out, or to cease to draw breath. *Nirvāṇa* is blown out, extinguished, like a lamp or fire, set as the sun, deceased with the fire of life extinguished, de-spirated. As a fire is quenched for want of fuel, so the flames of desire are blown out and peace is attained.

In the Bhagavad Gītā *nirvāṇa* is found in union with God: 'Intent on me . . . the yogi of restrained mind comes to the peace that is in me, the supreme *nirvāṇa*.' The goal is also spoken of as Brahma-nirvāṇa. Fixed in the divine state (*brāhmīsthiti*) at the hour of death one becomes Brahman or enters into Brahma-nirvāṇa. This could mean simply entering into an eternal mode of being, and this is the trend of the early chapters of the Gītā, but in the later chapters Kṛishṇa is recognized as 'the supreme Brahman and the supreme abode'.[12]

The ultimate goal, beyond this world and the many heavens, in the Upanishads and the *advaita* schools is merging in the divine. This is different from Buddhism or Jainism, which deny or ignore the divine Brahman. So the Praśna Upanishad says not only that as birds resort to a tree so does everything resort to the Supreme Soul (*paraātman*), but also that he who recognizes the pure imperishable attains to the Imperishable, and knowing all he becomes the All.[13]

The metaphors of the snake freeing itself from its skin, and the river running into the sea, are commonly used. Casting off name and shape (*nāma-rūpa*), the one who knows attains to the divine Person, higher than the high, and 'he who knows the supreme Brahman becomes very Brahman'. It does not necessarily mean that the river is lost in the ocean as a drop of no importance, but that it is only now truly conscious and aware of its oneness and infinity.[14]

Complete identity with the divine is the goal of this monistic teaching, and the final end and perfection of life. 'The infinite is happiness, there is no pleasure in anything small, only in the infinite.'[15]

The Gītā goes beyond this monism, and although in its early chapters it speaks of becoming one with Brahman (*brahmabhūtam*), and of infinite bliss in the eternal Brahman, in the later chapters the goal is more personalized. In his manifestation to Arjuna in infinite forms, Kṛishṇa is revealed as greater than Brahman, being and non-being, and what is beyond that. The frightened Arjuna seeks for grace and is comforted by the Exalted One. In the final chapter of the Gītā the yogi has become one with Brahman but then, through the grace of the Lord, and through devotion to him, he approaches the Lord. This is a new and secret doctrine, not to be spoken to one who has no devotion in him. It shows that the ultimate aim of existence, according to the Gītā, is not becoming Brahman but is union with the Lord, the beatific vision.

The Biblical view of the nature of life after death is not so detailed, or so crude, as much later popular Christian writing might suggest. There is, in fact, very little detail in the Bible on this subject, apart from the visions and dreams of the book of Revelation. This book became one of the chief sources of later fantasy, but its deliberate symbolism is to be understood in the light of earlier apocalyptic teaching in Daniel and Ezekiel. The many gradations of heaven, hell and purgatory that developed in medieval thought, and classically in Dante, and which recall the many heavens and hells of popular Hindu and Buddhist story, have little enough basis in the Bible.

The Old Testament idea of heaven was that it stretched out like a giant tent in the desert, though it was solid and borne up on pillars. Above it were the waters, rain, snow and hail, and in it the stars were fixed. There were heavens above the visible firmament, and in later times these were reckoned as three or seven. St. Paul spoke of one who was 'caught up to the third heaven'. But there could never be any doubt to the Hebrew mind that God was in the highest heaven, or above all. In the great prayer attributed to Solomon it is said that 'heaven and the heaven of heavens cannot contain thee'.[16]

We have seen that the dead were thought, in the Old Testament but not in the New, to be underneath the ground in Sheol. But at least one of the Psalms said that God was there too. Between the Testaments there was development, perhaps under Greek and Persian influence. So in the Book of Wisdom we read that 'the souls of the righteous are in the hand of God, and no torment shall touch them. In the eyes of the foolish they seem to have died . . . but they are in peace and their hope is full of immortality.' And again, 'the righteous live for ever, and in the Lord is their reward and the care for them with the Most High.... With his right hand shall he cover them, and with his arm shall he shield them.'[17] This clearly shows that the just are believed to have a personal relationship with God in heaven.

The Gospels attempt remarkably little description of life after death. Jesus said little about it, apart from affirming faith in the resurrection; God 'is not the God of the dead but of the living'. The word 'heaven' is used, of course, as a reverential substitute for the name of God. The kingdom of heaven means the kingdom or reign of God, not just a celestial heaven. Your heavenly Father means God, and so on. Heaven is the realm where God has perfect sway, and the Lord's Prayer asks that God's will may be done on earth as it is always done in heaven.

Occasionally Jesus used common metaphors about heaven in the sense of a future abode, but without giving particulars. So he spoke of the poor Lazarus being carried by angels to Abraham's bosom, while the rich man was tormented in the flames of Hades. This latter seems a combination of the ancient Sheol and the later Gehenna. Gehenna was the valley of Hinnom near Jerusalem, where once human sacrifices had been offered and then idols were burnt there, and so it became the city's dump and rubbish was always burning, 'where the worm dies not and the fire is not quenched'. This is a symbol of the outer darkness, away from God.[18]

The symbol of a banquet is used in the Gospels for heaven, to which many will come from east and west and sit down with the patriarchs, while the sons of the kingdom are cast into darkness. But this is a Messianic feast, and it may be on this earth in the millennium rather than being a description of eternal life in heaven.[19]

Jesus also once used the term Paradise, to the dying thief. This came from a Persian word for a garden, and in Jewish usage also referred to the Garden of Eden with its tree of life. The rabbis seem to have thought of two paradises, one in Sheol and one in heaven, and there were rabbinic speculations about the purpose of Paradise as a place of cleansing and preparation for heaven.

The righteous now in Paradise would rise again to judgement and then to heaven.

Jesus also spoke of death as sleep, concerning Jairus' daughter and Lazarus. And this was taken up by the church to show that Christian faith had removed the bitterness of death: Stephen in his violent martyrdom 'fell asleep'. Paul both speaks of those 'who have fallen asleep in Christ' already, and says that in future 'we shall not all sleep, but we shall all be changed'.[20]

Apart from these few references the main burden of New Testament teaching is in terms of eternal life. The unconditioned nature of the future life is stressed: 'they neither marry nor are given in marriage; neither can they die any more, for they are equal to the angels and are sons of God'.[21]

Eternal life is the goal of the righteous, and in the parable of the judgement eternal punishment is said to be the lot of the wicked. This is not necessarily everlastingness, but it is a state beyond time. The essence of the parable is the separation of the harsh and uncharitable from the merciful and kind. 'The New Testament does not answer the questions we like to ask about such matters as the nature of punishment after death, eternal retribution, and so on; and it is as much a mistake to erect its symbolic language into metaphysical answers as it is to ignore the solemnity of the warnings which that language conveys'.[22]

The most profound teaching about eternal life is developed in the Fourth Gospel. Christ came that 'whosoever believes in him should not perish but have eternal life'. This is not just a future state, but can be a present condition, for 'he that believes on the Son has eternal life' now. Similarly judgement is not merely a future event but a present result. 'He that believes him that sent me has eternal life, and comes not into judgement but has passed from death to life.' This leads straight on to the declaration, 'I am the resurrection and the life . . . whosoever lives and believes in me shall never die'.[23]

Both faith and knowledge are involved in the apprehension of eternal life. Indeed it is so defined: 'this is eternal life, that they should know thee, the only true God, and him whom thou didst send, even Jesus Christ'.[24] To know is to perceive the truth, after hearing the word, and to believe in the truth. But those who reject revealed truth are self-condemned and love darkness rather than light.

But more than faith and knowledge are needed, else this might be a solitary or selfish experience. The epistle of John goes on to emphasize the necessity of love to others. You cannot love the unseen God if you do not love your seen brother. And so 'we have passed out of death into life, because we love the brethren'. Love is the key to life and death and eternal life.[25]

This not only links up with the teaching of the Synoptic Gospels on eternal life as the gift of God to the merciful and kind, but it applies also to the whole manner of the life and death of Jesus. 'He laid down his life for us, and we ought to lay down our lives for the brethren.' The strong moral, social and self-sacrificing trend of Biblical thought and living finds its climax here.[26]

Eternal life, in Biblical teaching, is not the flight of the alone to the Alone, but life in the redeemed community. This qualifies even the most intimate statements about the relationship of the soul to God. The Bible knows nothing of the identity of man with God. Union is expressed, but not identity. Paul says, 'I live, and yet no longer I, but Christ lives in me.' That might appear to be identity, but he immediately qualifies it by showing that not only is he speaking of life still here in the body, but also of a dependent relationship of faith to Christ. 'That life which I now live in the flesh I live by faith in the Son of God.'[27]

Similarly Paul speaks of the new Christian life as itself a resurrection, and a communal one. 'He raised us up with him [Christ], and made us sit with him in heavenly places.' This is a present experience, though a foretaste or earnest of things to come.[28]

The Christian goal is this eternal life, which can begin now and transcend death. It is in communion with God, and its condition is love both to God and man. The colourful pictures of heaven in Revelation are but symbols of the deeper eternal reality when God will be all in all. The apprehension of this in the beatific vision of mysticism will be treated of later.

References

1. Kaushītaki Upanishad 1, 2–4.
2. Kaṭha 1 ff.
3. Chāndogya 8, 4.
4. ib. 8, 13; Muṇḍaka 1, 2, 5; 3, 2, 6.
5. Taittirīya 3, 10, 5.
6. Chānd. 8, 3, 2.
7. Bṛihad-āraṇyaka 4, 4, 2; Muṇḍ. 3, 2, 6.
8. Maitri 6, 30.
9. Praśna 5; Muṇḍ. 3, 2, 6.
10. Śvetāśvatara 6, 16–18; Gītā 10, 3. Rāmānuja, quoted in *Hindu and Muslim Mysticism*, p. 193.
11. Maitri 6, 22.
12. Bhagavad Gītā 6, 15; 2, 72; 5, 24 f.; 14, 27.
13. Praśna 4, 7 ff.
14. Muṇḍ. 3, 2, 8 f.
15. Chānd. 7, 23.
16. 2 Cor. 12, 2; 1 Kings 8, 27.
17. Wisdom 3, 1 f.; 5, 15 f.
18. Luke 16, 19 ff.; Mark 9, 47 f.
19. Matthew 8, 11 f.
20. Mark 5, 39; John 11, 11; Acts 7, 60; 1 Cor. 15, 20, 51.
21. Luke 20, 36.
22. Matt. 25, 46. A. Richardson, *Theological Word Book*, p. 107.
23. John 3, 16; 3, 36; 5, 24; 11, 25.
24. ib. 17, 3.
25. 1 John 3, 14.
26. ib. 3, 16.
27. Gal. 2, 20.
28. Eph. 2, 6.

Chapter 7

THE DISCIPLINE OF THE SPIRITUAL LIFE

Unity with the divine, Brahman-ātman, is the supreme goal of the Upanishads, and theoretically this is obtainable by knowledge alone. So we read that 'he who has found and awakened to the Soul . . . he is the maker of everything . . . the world is his'. And again, 'wise men, free from desires, worship the Person, and pass beyond the seed of rebirth'. And we are twice told that the Brahmins who have known the soul rise above desires and have no more wishes, even for children: 'what need have we of offspring, whose soul is the universe?'[1]

Yet desires keep arising, and the practices of *yoga* set out to harness the senses and the thoughts from false and manifold objects and bring about union with the one universal soul.

Mircea Eliade, in his study of *yoga*, speaks of 'four basic and interdependent concepts, four "kinetic ideas" [which] bring us directly to the core of Indian spirituality. They are *karma*, *māyā*, *nirvāṇa*, and *yoga*. . . . The means of attaining to Being, the effectual techniques for gaining liberation. This corpus of means constitutes Yoga properly speaking.'[2]

The word *yoga* comes from a root (*yuj*) meaning to bind together, to hold fast, or to yoke. Our English word 'yoke' is from the same root, and this should help to understand the binding and disciplining content of the word (so also Latin *jugum*, and French *joug*).

The word Yoga can be used generally of any ascetic method or technique of meditation and concentration, and there have been great varieties of these in the different Indian religious and philosophical movements. There is a classical Yoga, which is closely linked with the Sāṁkhya system of philosophy, but there are many popular and less systematic forms, and others outside Hinduism, in Buddhism and Jainism. And there are popular varieties which are mainly magical and 'mystical', whose adepts seek after *siddhis*: supernatural powers, telepathy, clairvoyance, breath-control, digestion-control, levitation, flying through the air, conjuring tricks, burial alive, and so on. Of these the classical systems say little, and regard them with scorn as inferior occupations for charlatans and those at a spiritually low level.

The term Yoga itself may be partly responsible for this wide variety of meanings, for though it means binding and discipline, yet the self-mastery implied would seem to free one from normal human limitations and bind one to the spirit world. Hence the adept may claim mastery of the body and of the whole world, assume divine powers, and pretend to omniscience and omnipotence. But the philosophical and devotional Yoga schools should look primarily for isolation or union of the soul with the divine.

Yoga is a very old practice in India, as the variety of its methods already mentioned suggests. One of the most important discoveries in the Indus Valley excavations was a seal with a representation of a being sitting in a yoga posture. Sir John Marshall thus described him, 'The God, who is three-faced, is seated on a low Indian throne in a typical attitude of Yoga, with legs bent double beneath him, heel to heel, and toes turned downwards.' And Stuart Piggott commented, 'There can be little doubt that we have here the prototype of the great god Shiva as Lord of the Beasts and Prince of Yogis.' Other seals also have representations of beings in the sitting position, and another statue also resembles a yogi; as Marshall put it, 'it represents someone seemingly in the pose of a yogi, and it is for this reason that the eyelids are more than half closed and the eyes looking downward to the tip of the nose'.[3]

This means that yogic practices were already well known in the time of the Indus civilization (about 2500–1500 B.C.). There is little trace of them in the Ṛig Vedic hymns, and only gradual development of yogic ideas in the Upanishads, but full recognition in the Bhagavad Gītā. This shows again that submergence of ancient Indian ideas and then reappearance at a later date which we noticed earlier in speaking of transmigration, and which seems also to apply to the worship of deities such as Śiva, Kṛishṇa and the Great Goddess.

This conclusion is strengthened by a brief consideration of the philosophy that came to be associated with Yoga. Yoga deals with methods of disentanglement of the soul from embodiment, and it puts out practical ways for gaining release or 'isolation-integration'. But it is closely linked with the Sāṁkhya philosophy. Sāṁkhya means 'enumeration', and it is an analysis of human nature, enumerating and defining its different elements, describing their entanglement in existence and considering the way of liberation (*moksha*). The method of gaining this is set out as Yoga.

These ideas are not found in the early Vedic texts nor, on the other hand, are the many gods of the Ṛig Veda found in the basic teachings of Sāṁkhya and Yoga. They can proceed without any gods as methods of self-discipline and liberation, since Sāṁkhya is a quest for bliss, seeking after isolation. But it is recommended that there should be a 'god of one's choice' (*iṣṭa-devatā*) who is a help to concentration. And the Yoga-sūtras speak of one Lord (*Īśvara*) who is the object of contemplation, the pattern of the isolated soul and, in some writers, the object of devotion.

It may well be that the Yoga systems go back to Indus times, and are independent of the Vedas, but come to infiltrate the later Vedānta. Sāṁkhya is believed to have been founded by a sage called Kapila. He is not known to the Vedas, but he does occur in the epic poem, the Mahābhārata, sitting in meditation deep in the bowels of the earth and burning intruders to ashes with a flash of his eye.

The classical textbook of the Yoga system is the Yoga-sūtras of Patañjali. These are very short, pithy sentences, which try to sum up a great mass of material current at the time, and give Yoga a theoretical basis. The four short books were apparently composed some shortly before and some after the beginning of the Christian era. The association of Sāṁkhya and Yoga was clearly known to the Gītā, for it says that 'puerile and unlearned people speak of Sāṁkhya and Yoga as distinct from each other, yet anyone firmly established in either gains the fruit of both. . . . He truly sees who regards them as one.'[4]

Looking now to the Vedas we see that there is no clear Yoga in the Ṛig Vedic hymns. We do read of an ascetic (*muni*), long-haired, dressed in yellow, flying through the air, and into whom the gods enter. But this may be an ecstatic, the like of whom is found in many ancient religions.

In the Upanishads knowledge and contemplation are the chief means whereby identity of Brahman and *ātman* are perceived, but some yogic methods are accepted as exercises leading to purification. There is a great mass of later Upanishads commonly known as Yoga Upanishads, which accept full yogic disciplines, and either declare 'I am the transcendent Brahman . . . extolled by all the gods'; or else dispense with all worship, 'Ablution, silent prayer, penance, offering oblation, the study of the Veda, the worship of the tutelary deity . . . all this is falsehood.'[5]

But in the older classical Upanishads yogic practices only find occasional mention, such as 'concentrating all the senses upon one's self', and there is some practice of breath-control. In the Kaṭha and Taittirīya Upanishads Yoga is first clearly spoken of, 'the Yoga-study of what pertains to self'.[6]

A key passage is the descent of the youth Nachiketas into Hades, his visit to Yama (Death). In the third question which Nachiketas presses Death to answer, the all-important problem of the great passing-on, it is significant that Death reveals the knowledge of the eternal soul and the method of Yoga together. The turbulent nature of the body is well known; the senses are horses, the body is the chariot, the mind is the charioteer, and the soul is lord of the chariot. So the mind must always be restrained and the senses under control. The Upanishad goes on to speak of Yoga as the firm holding back of the senses, by which one becomes distracted. The highest state is reached when the five senses and the mind cease from their normal activities, when the intellect does not stir, but the soul undistracted perceives the unmanifested supreme Person. So Nachiketas, having received this knowledge declared by Death, and the entire rule of Yoga, attained Brahman and became free from passion and from death.[7]

In other old Upanishads we find teaching developing about the practices or postures of Yoga. Thus the Maitri enumerates a sixfold Yoga for attaining unity with Brahman. These are: restraint of breath (*prāṇāyāma*), withdrawal of the senses (*pratyāhāra*), meditation (*dhyāna*), concentration (*dhāraṇā*), contemplation or reflection (*tarka*), and absorption (*samādhi*). Such is said to be the sixfold Yoga. The later Rāja Yoga has eight limbs or practices.

Particularly interesting, in view of later yogic exercises, is the higher concentration (*dhāraṇā*), whereby it is said that 'by pressing the tip of the tongue against the palate, by restraining voice, mind, and breath, one sees Brahman through contemplation' (*tarka*).

The next paragraph speaks of breath-control, and meditation on the syllable Om. Several other passages emphasize that meditation on Om leads to deliverance, and brings union with Brahman and immortality.

The shortest of all the older Upanishads, the Māṇḍūkya, of only twelve verses, devotes itself to the mysterious syllable Om. This is split up into the three letters A, U, M and the final synthesis Om. (o is a diphthong made up of a and u, and so Om can also be written Aum, and the silence following and surrounding the utterance of the syllable was said to make a fourth part in the interpretation of it.) Meditation on Om is traceable already in the Vedas. It shows the importance attached to auditory helps to meditation, in the microscopic interpretations of the word. 'Om, this syllable is the whole world . . . past, present, and future, everything is just the word Om. . . . This Om is the *ātman*, he who knows this with his self enters the Self.'[8]

In the more theistic of the classical Upanishads Yoga takes on a more religious air, and the Lord appears as object of contemplation. In the Kaṭha we read that 'he who has understanding as a chariot-driver, who reins in his mind, he reaches the end of his journey, that highest place of Vishṇu'. It is interesting that Vishṇu appears here as Lord, where Yoga and immortality are in question.[9]

In the Śvetāśvatara Upanishad the impersonal Brahman is represented by Śiva (Rudra) as the Lord (Bhagavat). By the efficacy of his austerity, and the grace of the god (*devaprasāda*), the sage Śvetāśvatara spoke about Brahman to the seers. He taught three basic yogic practices: sitting posture (*āsana*), withdrawal of the senses (*pratyāhāra*), and breath-control (*prāṇāyāma*). 'Holding the body steady with the three upper parts erect . . . having repressed his breathings here in the body, and having his movements checked, one should breathe through his nostrils with diminished breath. The wise man should restrain his mind undistractedly, like that chariot yoked with vicious horses. In a clean level spot, free from pebbles, fire and gravel . . . In a hidden retreat protected from the wind, one should practise Yoga.'[10]

Having given the technique it then goes on to say that one is cleansed as a mirror is freed from dust, and so 'a practitioner of Yoga beholds here the very nature of Brahman. . . . By knowing God one is released from all fetters.' This refrain comes in again and again, 'by knowing God one is released from all fetters'. The purpose of Yoga now appears as knowledge of God, and not just self-discipline or isolated salvation. This leads on to the Gītā.

The Bhagavad Gītā has often been called the highest point of Indian spirituality. It is also a great attempt at a synthesis of different traditions, and to this it owes a good deal of its success. The Gītā gives Yoga a high place, and it is expounded and recommended by Kṛishṇa to Arjuna. But it is Yoga with a difference. It is far removed from the popular yogic techniques which tried to gain magical results and superhuman powers. While the Gītā presents a popular faith, accessible even to women and to the low-caste Śūdras, yet it firmly ignores vulgar cravings after magic.

On the other hand, the Gītā also differs from the Yoga teaching of Patañjali. It both simplifies the methods recommended, and sets out its own goal of devotion to God which conditions all its teaching. As a great synthesis it tries to bring the varying yogas or paths to salvation into line with the way of devotion.

The Gītā is called 'the scripture of Yoga' (*yoga-śāstra*), and from the second chapter it expounds 'the wisdom of yoga' which will help the hearer to get rid of the bondage of works (*karma*). A great contribution of the Gītā to Indian thought is its insistence that work must be done, but its bondage is broken by non-attachment (see Chapter 9 below). So the warrior is told, 'fixed in yoga, do thy work, abandoning attachment, with an even mind, for this is yoga indeed'. The yoking of intelligence is far superior to mere action, or seeking the fruits of action, and the one with yoked intelligence even now has cast away both good and evil. Such a one passes beyond delusions, is firm in contemplation (*samādhi*), and attains to insight. All the senses having been brought under control, he should remain firm in yoga, intent on God.[11]

Chapter 3 deals with two ways of yoga which had been taught in earlier times: the Yoga of knowledge (*jñāna-yoga*), and the Yoga of works (*karma-yoga*). The former was for men of contemplation, the latter for men of action. And it goes on to justify action from the very activity of the Lord himself. The next chapter is careful to point out that this imperishable Yoga is no new doctrine, having been taught to the ancient seers, including Manu. But it was lost to the world by a long lapse of time (perhaps during the oppression of the Indus peoples). Kṛishṇa had many lives, some of them before the days of the oldest sages, and whenever there is a decline of righteousness (*dharma*) and a growth of unrighteousness, then he manifests himself and comes into being through his own power (*māyā*). To protect the good and establish order (*dharma*) Kṛishṇa comes into being from age to age.[12]

The Gītā gives approval to both Yogas, activity and contemplation, as equally valid paths to salvation. Thus it solves a dilemma that puzzled other thinkers, by showing that either method of Yoga may be followed, according to the present situation of the individual. Hence Kṛishṇa is Lord of Yoga (*Yogeśvara*) and he shows the way to right and victory. Yet between the two Yogas, the unselfish performance of works is thought to be better than complete renunciation of activity, for in fact it is impossible to be completely inactive and not work at all.[13]

But the Gītā constantly strains after a yet higher form of Yoga. Even when the seeker is urged to bring all his senses under control, he should be intent on God. And when Chapter 6 describes the method of Yoga it ends with the mind turned to God, intent on him alone, and so attaining to peace, the supreme *nirvāṇa*, which abides in him.[14]

The Gītā gives a brief technique of Yoga, which resembles that of Patañjali, but is simpler and more truly theistic. There is no mention of breath-control or similar practices. The yogi should sit in a clean place, neither too high nor too low, on a firm seat of grass and deerskin. He should control sense and thought, and make his mind one-pointed. The body is to be erect and still, the eyes fixed on the tip of the nose without wandering round. Then, serene and fearless, steadfastly thinking on God, he must practise Yoga, taking God as the supreme end.[15]

In Sāṁkhya-Yoga the Lord (*Īśvara*) appears simply as an aid to Yoga, and may later be dispensed with; a thought that is shocking to people of monotheistic religions. But in the later chapters of the Gītā Kṛishṇa is the sole object of concentration, the only goal, and it is through his grace that the yogi attains to the *nirvāṇa* that here is the union of the soul and God. Thus the Yoga of devotion (*bhakti-yoga*) is held up as superior to meditation on the Absolute and the search for the Unmanifested. Those who fix their minds on God are 'the most perfect in Yoga'. The devotee (*bhakta*) is dear to God, who takes pity on him and shows him grace. So the final command is, 'fix thy mind on me, be devoted to me . . . so shalt thou come to me, for thou art dear to me'.[16]

This is both the triumph and the transformation of Yoga. It is elevated to a high place, yet purged from magical associations, but it is subservient to devotion. So Indian devotion accepted Yoga as a means of obtaining mystical 'union' with a personal God. The great development that this underwent in the later Bhakti literature of the followers of Vishṇu is beyond our scope here.

It might well seem that the Bible has little to compare with such energetic spiritual techniques as have developed in India. In part this assumption would be western prejudice. We all read the Bible, as Schweitzer once said, through coloured spectacles: liberal, fundamentalist or, in his own case, eschatological. The western Protestant, in particular, may find it hard to realize that Hebrews and Christians in many ages spent much time and effort in the cultivation of the spiritual life. The eastern Churches understand this better, and they are nearer to Palestine and India.

A number of men in the Old Testament retired from the world for lengthy periods, or undertook arduous discipline for their spiritual life. Moses withdrew to the wilderness, not only at the time of his first experience of God, but constantly to Sinai and elsewhere to receive the divine word. In a later age Elijah, a man from semi-desert country in Transjordan, spent three years by the brook with the wild ravens.

Most of the prophets undertook ascetic practices at times. They were rather wild men, and not the worldly statesmen that modern thought has often pictured. Jeremiah went about the streets wearing a yoke on his neck (a muscular type of yoga!). Ezekiel shaved off his hair and laid for a long time on his side. While Isaiah is said to have walked about naked for three years.

Any man or woman could make the vow of a Nazirite (a separated or consecrated person to God), either for life or temporarily. Samson did not cut his hair or drink wine. The ordinary Nazirite had to observe these taboos, and also keep himself from unclean things and persons. 'All the days of his separation he is holy to the Lord.'[17]

Although the Hebrews disliked celibacy and the extremes of monasticism, yet we know that there were monasteries or community centres of the Essene sect in New Testament times. The Dead Sea scrolls belonged to one such monastery. The Essenes, though usually married, were said to be strict in their sexual and food regulations.

John the Baptist was a man of the desert, like Elijah. Jesus, after his baptism, retired to the desert for forty days; and at other times in his ministry he withdrew from the crowds, either getting up in the night for prayer or leaving the country with his disciples. Paul after his conversion went away into Arabia before beginning his ministry.[18]

The practice of fasting was often observed. Joel called the people to a collective fast, with weeping and mourning. Tearing the clothes and sitting in sackcloth and ashes is common in the Old Testament. But the prophets insisted that the outward signs were less important than inward repentance: 'Rend your hearts and not your garments, and turn unto the Lord your God.' The true fast is to give bread to the hungry and bring the poor into your house. The ethical side of religion was always prominent.[19]

So in the New Testament fasting, while recommended with prayer for spiritual advancement, should be in secret, not with unsightly faces to catch the attention of men, but with outward appearance well groomed yet with inward fasting to be seen by God alone.[20]

The Biblical emphasis, as a strongly personal religion, is on prayer above all. There is never any suggestion of spiritual training for its own sake, any more than art for art's sake, or simply for self-improvement. It begins where the Gītā ends, with man's regard turned towards God and no spirituality apart from him.

Yet prayer is to be inward and it needs discipline. It is not to be displayed in public, or done in order to gain credit for holiness, or yet to consist of constant repetitions, for God knows what is needed. But the disciple is told to 'go into a room by yourself, shut the door, and pray to your Father who is there in the secret place'.[21]

Silent prayer and meditation have sunk to a low place in modern western Protestantism, and this partly accounts for the appeal of eastern devotion and Yoga. However, in the religious communities and in the devotions of serious laity, both Eastern Orthodox and Roman Catholics practise meditation and spiritual disciplines. In Protestantism the Quakers approach nearest to Indian ways, in their practice of silence.

Even so, it must be agreed that the Bible does not set out any regular methods of body and mind control such as were so highly developed in Indian yoga. As a religion which paid great attention to the material, the Bible was well aware of the temptations of the flesh and the need to discipline it. St. Paul, in particular, says that the body is a temple of the Holy Spirit and therefore must be kept pure; 'glorify God in your body'. He urges men to 'present your bodies a living sacrifice to God'. He takes the example of athletes for self-restraint, 'every athlete goes into strict training'. Of himself he said, 'I keep under my body and bring it into subjection.' Of his trials under persecution he said that he 'always bore about in his body the dying of Jesus', and made up what was lacking of the sufferings of Christ.[22] With the example of the death of Jesus before them, the early Christians never expected an easy life and underwent persecution as a normal part of their religion. In this Christianity has an acceptance of hardship that is absent in some other religions.

There is no clearly worked out Christian yoga. We are urged by Jesus to 'take my yoke upon you', and it has been suggested that the words 'take up your cross' might originally have been 'take up your yoke'. On self-control and discipline there is plenty of teaching; self-sacrifice, for Christ and the Gospel, for one's friends, even for enemies. All these are taught. But Christianity is essentially a way of devotion (*bhakti-mārga*). The stress is on prayer, devotion and adoration. But mental prayer, fasting, retreats, and meditation may all be used if they serve the end of devotion to God. In later Christianity the use of prayer beads, the repetition of sacred texts, the invocation of the Name, the Jesus-prayer, all served to discipline mind and body.

There is no teaching in the Bible on breath-control, posture of meditation, fixing of the gaze, inaction, one-pointedness of mind. Here indeed the Christian West may learn from the East now, for former ages had virtually no knowledge of Indian religions and their devotional practices. As R. C. Zaehner has said, 'It is more natural that we should learn from the Indians than from the Greeks', for India was so much more advanced than Greece in spiritual techniques.

Father Déchanet's *Christian Yoga* shows one way of using Indian methods and investing them with a Christian meaning. Some may doubt whether this is possible, or legitimate. If it is at all possible then Christian teaching that is true to the Bible would ensure, as the Gītā does, that the yogic methods it takes over are subordinated to the supreme end of devotion to God.[23]

In these days of anxiety and rush one attraction of Indian methods of body and mind control is that peace which it is hoped to find thereby. Yet this may point back to the Gospel, one of whose most neglected commands is 'do not be anxious . . . these are things for the heathen to run after. . . . Set your mind on God's kingdom and justice and all the rest will come to you as well.' And one of the final Biblical blessings is that 'the peace of God which passes all understanding, will keep your hearts and thoughts'.[24]

References

1. Bṛihad-āraṇyaka Upanishad 4, 4, 13; 4, 4, 22; Muṇḍaka 3, 2, 1.
2. *Yoga, Immortality and Freedom*, p. 3.
3. *Mohenjo-daro and the Indus Civilization*, 1, 52; 1, 44, 54. *Prehistoric India*, p. 202.
4. Bhagavad Gītā 5, 4–5.
5. Tejo-bindu Upanishad 4, 31; 5, 50 f.
6. Taittirīya 2, 4; Kaṭha 2, 12; Chāndogya 8, 15; Bṛih. 1, 5, 23.
7. Kaṭha 2, 12; 6, 18.
8. Maitri 6, 18; Māṇḍūkya 1, 12.
9. Kaṭha 3, 9; Maitri 6, 23.
10. Śvetāśvatara 2, 8–10.
11. Gītā 2, 48–9; 2, 53–61.
12. ib. 3, 3; 4, 1–8.
13. ib. 5, 2.
14. ib. 2, 61; 6, 14 f.
15. ib. 6, 11–14.
16. ib. 12, 2; 18, 65.
17. Numbers 6, 2 ff.
18. Galatians 1, 17.
19. Joel 2, 13 f.; Isaiah 58, 6.

20. Matthew 6, 16 f.
21. ib. 6, 6 (*New English Bible*).
22. 1 Cor. 6, 19; Romans 12; 1 Cor. 9, 24 ff.; 2 Cor. 4, 10; Col. 1, 24.
23. *Christian Yoga* (E.T., Burns & Oates, 1960).
24. Matt. 6, 31f. (*N.E.B.*); Phil. 4, 7.

Chapter 8

MYSTICISM

Mysticism is such a popular and confusing subject that one has to proceed warily, and define the terms used, as far as possible. The great variety of books on mysticism range from the mysterious and occult to treatises on the love of God in catholic devotion. In loose talk about it eastern religions are often said to be mystical, and thereby superior, and the western unmystical. This is both misleading and untrue.

In origin the word 'mystic' is related to the Greek 'mystery', probably from a root meaning to close the lips or eyes. This secret mysterious air hangs around mysticism still.

In its definition of mysticism the *Shorter Oxford English Dictionary* makes two points; let us take the second first. The mystic is one 'who believes in the spiritual apprehension of truths inaccessible to the understanding'. Now it is true that the claim is often made that the mystic perceives truths which the reason cannot achieve or grasp. But it is doubtful how far this claim can be maintained. In all apprehension of truth the understanding must play some part, if only in the recognition of the truth when it appears. What is meant is probably that conscious reflection and reasoning are not obvious. Then truths flash upon the mind, which recognizes and accepts them, as if they came from nowhere. One person might say that they come from the subconscious mind (that great inexplicable), another that they come from God, or the universal mind. Similar flashes of inspiration are common in science, and are the special material of poet and artist.

But religious mysticism is surely something more than a different kind of knowledge. The definition first given in the dictionary is that the mystic is 'one who seeks by contemplation and self-surrender to obtain union with or absorption into the Deity'. This is more to the point, and the great difference between various kinds of religious or 'sacred' mysticism is indicated by the alternatives 'union with or absorption into' the Deity. The 'profane' mysticism, of drugs, drink or madness, illustrated in Aldous Huxley's *Doors of Perception*, is beyond our subject here.

One of the most discriminating studies of the Indian texts is S. N. Dasgupta's *Hindu Mysticism*, and to this must be added R. C. Zaehner's outstanding works, *Mysticism, Sacred and Profane*, and *Hindu and Muslim Mysticism*. Dasgupta distinguishes six types of mysticism in India which he calls: Sacrificial Mysticism, Upanishadic Mysticism, Yoga Mysticism, Buddhistic Mysticism, Classical Devotional Mysticism, and Popular Devotional Mysticism. This classification is made historically, but the last two at least overlap, and the right of the first to be called mysticism may be questioned.

Dasgupta calls Sacrificial Mysticism the practices of the priests in the old Vedic times, as reflected in the Ṛig Vedic hymns and Brāhmaṇas. These were especially concerned with the exact performance of sacrificial ritual, by which the priests hoped to gain secret powers that would bring about present or future effects. This might be called magical mysticism, and it is often looked on as an inferior thing in the Upanishads. But the Vedic hymns also contain expressions of devotion that might be the germs of more theistic mysticism. The sun (Pūshan) is besought, 'accept with favour this my song, be gracious to the earnest thought even as a bridegroom to his bride'. And the great god Varuṇa, in particular, is prayed to earnestly, 'Cast our sins away like loosened fetters, and let us be thine own beloved.' And the famous Gāyatrī *mantra*, the verse which is called 'the mother of the Vedas', expresses a yearning for the divine, 'Let us meditate on the adorable glory of the radiant sun [Savitṛi], may he stimulate our prayers.'[1]

In the Upanishads there is a deeper search for the heart of

reality. By knowledge and ascetic life men seek the highest mysteries, looking for the liberation (*moksha*) of the soul from the conditions of its mortal state and its entry into unconditioned eternity. There are different trends in the Upanishads, however, as we have noticed before on other subjects. Dasgupta says that the chief features of Upanishadic mysticism are 'the earnest and sincere quest for this spiritual illumination, the rapturous delight and force that characterize the utterance of the sages when they speak of the realization of this ineffable experience. . . . Yet this quest is not the quest of the God of the theists. This highest reality is no individual person separate from us. . . . It is, rather, a totality of partless, simple and undifferentiated experience which is the root of all our ordinary knowledge and experience, and which is at once the ultimate essence of our self, the highest principle of the universe, the Brahman or the Atman.'[2]

The identity of the soul and the divine is taught again and again in the Upanishads. It is the meaning of the great refrain 'that thou art' (*tat tvam asi*), and is the basis of the non-dualistic philosophy of Śaṅkara. It might be argued that leaving out 'the God of the theists' ('dropping the Object', as C. E. M. Joad called it) could mean the death of religion. The identity of human and divine could make religious language meaningless, and it seems tautology to say that the *ātman* is the same as the Brahman. Does this not mean finally 'I am I', and lead to the solipsist conclusion, 'I am all, naught else exists'? Yet we have seen that not only do great Upanishadic commentators such as Rāmānuja and Madhva strongly dissent from this, but even Śaṅkara admits the presence of *māyā* and so restores a kind of relationship within the divine.

There is a considerable difference between the Upanishads on the one hand, and 'Yogic Mysticism' and 'Buddhistic Mysticism' on the other. The Yoga Sūtras do indeed allow for the existence of a god, but the goal of the classical yoga systems is not union with the divine, but the isolation of the human soul, and the realization of its eternity outside space and time. The ultimate stage, says Dasgupta, is when the 'self will shine forth in its own light and he himself will be absolutely free in bondless, companionless loneliness of self-illumination'.[3] This is akin to the Buddhist *nirvāṇa*, except that in Buddhism not only is there no God, but no self either; at least not in what seems to be the original teaching, though later Buddhism, especially Mahāyāna, introduced many divine objects of devotion and varied its no-soul idea.

But the classical Upanishads throughout believe in liberation, into complete harmony and union with the divine. This is the mysticism of 'absorption into the Deity'. And then there is the second great line of Hindu thought in which a theistic belief is presented in a personal God, who is the source of all things and the object of devotion. Dasgupta says that the Upanishadic authors oscillated between different phases of experience and belief, sometimes believing in a great Creator, sometimes in a blissful experience itself, and sometimes simply in a unity wherein all duality has vanished. But it is significant that the more theistic Upanishads are the later ones in the classical series and lead on to the Bhagavad Gītā.[4]

In the Taittirīya Upanishad we read, 'Into thee thyself, O Gracious Lord, may I enter. . . . Do thou thyself enter into me. . . . In thee I am cleansed. . . . Thou art a refuge. Shine upon me. Come unto me!' The Īśa, Kena, Kaṭha and Muṇḍaka Upanishads all have some theistic lines, and the Śvetāśvatara carries the process to the conclusion of teaching devotion to God. 'To him who of old creates Brahmā, and who, verily, delivers to him the Vedas, to that God, lighted by his own intellect, do I, eager for liberation, resort for refuge.'[5]

Here the personal Lord takes pre-eminence. 'He who is the supreme Lord [*Maheśvara*] of lords, the supreme divinity of divinities, the supreme ruler of rulers, transcendent, him let us know as God, the Lord of the world, the adorable.' Some sages discourse of nature or time as the First Cause; deluded men, it is by the greatness of God that this wheel is caused to revolve. So the supreme truths and the mystery of the end of the Veda (Vedānta) are revealed to those who have devotion to God. 'To one who has the highest devotion [*bhakti*] to God . . . these matters which have been declared shine forth.'[6]

In the Bhagavad Gītā the 'Classical Devotional Mysticism' arises from faith in a personal God, who shows grace to his devoted follower. The latter is particularly important. Grace, or graciousness, from God finds occasional mention earlier. The idea is perhaps present in the Hymn of the Word in the Ṛig Veda, 'I make the man I love exceeding mighty.' In the Kaṭha Upanishad we read that 'this soul (*ātman*) is not to be obtained by instruction, nor by intellect, nor by much learning; he is to be obtained only . . . through the grace [*prasāda*] of the Creator'. So also in the Śvetāśvatara, 'One beholds him [the soul] as being without the human will, and becomes freed from sorrow—when through the grace of the Creator he sees the Lord and his greatness.'[7]

Generally, however, the Upanishadic teaching is that man should imitate God in detachment. The theistic texts see God as a perfect model, yet attachment to him in the sense of clinging or grasping would be a hindrance to liberation and detachment.

The Gītā wrestled with these problems, admitting the detachment and the virtues of Sāṁkhya-Yoga. But 'cheerfulness was always breaking in'. It followed at first the common teaching of the need for liberation, and recommended the technique of Yoga as a means of obtaining it. By his own efforts, it seemed, the yogi could gain liberation and the condition of Brahman. 'With thy mind integrated with the yoga of renunciation, thou shalt be freed from the good and evil fruits which are the bonds of action, and find release' (but also 'come to me'). And again, 'having become Brahman [*Brahmabhūta*], and serene in soul, he neither grieves nor desires, and is indifferent to all beings'.[8]

But being liberated, and become Brahman, what then? Is this the end, merging in the all, or nothingness? Not at all. Both these texts, and many others, are completed with what, to the Gītā, is the decisive step, the turning to God. 'Having become liberated, thou wilt draw nigh unto me.' And again, 'having become Brahman . . . he receives the supreme devotion to me'. So for the Gītā the realization of the immortality of the soul is only the preliminary to communion with God. This is going in the opposite direction to the Semitic religions, which put relationship to God first and the immortality of the soul as a gracious consequence of it.

The Gītā is slowly and finally orientated towards God and devotion to him, and this was to prove a powerful guide to the later devotional schools, the 'Popular Devotional Mysticism' of the Middle Ages and later. The great theophany of Chapter 11 of the Gītā opens the way. Having heard divine truths declared by Kṛishṇa, Arjuna wishes to go further and asks to see the divine form (like Moses before him). This is made possible by giving him the supernatural eye, and then Kṛishṇa reveals himself: 'The great Lord of Yoga [*mahāyogeśvara*] then revealed to Arjuna his supreme and divine form.'[9]

Forms and symbols are used, for in the worship of the personal God symbolism is indispensable. God is the imperishable, he is being and non-being, and what is beyond that. But some symbol is required lest the mind envisage God only vaguely, for the goal of the unmanifested is hard to reach by embodied beings. In later ages Dattātreya asked, 'How can I bow to him who is formless and undifferentiated?' And Tulsīdās said, 'the worship of the impersonal laid no hold on my heart'.[10]

The Gītā challenges those who dislike the worship of a personal God or the concept of an avatar or 'incarnate' divinity by saying, 'the deluded despise me clad in human body, not knowing my higher nature as great lord of all beings'. In fact, it says, all people worship God, whether as devout 'bowing down with devotion', or as learned, 'others again worship with the sacrifice of knowledge and regard me as the One'. There are differing ways of worship according to the individual; 'the faith of every man is according to his nature'.[11]

Nevertheless when Chapter 12 asks which way is better, the personal or the impersonal, the Gītā comes down strongly for the former. The way of the Unmanifested is hard, though men who succeed in it come to God just like the others. But those who worship in faith are the most perfect in Yoga, and God delivers them straightaway from the ocean of death-bound existence. In his commentary on the Gītā, Rāmānuja says that the yogi who worships with faith is more integrated than all others, and compared with him they are like a lot of mustard seeds beside Mount Meru.[12]

The grace of God to men, which appears a little in the Upanishads, comes to clearer light in the Gītā. And it now develops beyond condescension, into pity and love. Arjuna, having seen the fearful manifestations of God, is filled with a proper fear and (like Job at a similar theophany) 'bowing down and prostrating my body before thee, adorable Lord, I seek thy grace [*prasāda*].... Bear with me as a father to his son, as a friend to his friend, as a lover to his beloved.' At this plea Krishna responds, 'Be not afraid', and having taken again the form of grace he comforted the frightened warrior.[13]

It must have been hard to introduce the idea of a compassionate God into the Hindu conception of Brahman, for the latter is unaffected by any creatures and could not be subject to feelings of any kind. Earlier in the Gītā itself God is said to be 'alike' and 'indifferent' to all beings; 'none is hateful or dear to me'. On this Radhakrishnan comments, 'God has no friends or foes . . . the only way to win his love is by faith and devotion.'[14]

But the Gītā slowly modifies this view, and in the next chapter it says that God has compassion on those who love him, and while remaining impassive in his eternal nature, he yet delivers souls from darkness. In his lower nature he keeps the wheel of transmigration going, but he lifts devout souls out of the wheel.[15]

The devotee (*bhakta*) is dear to God, 'exceedingly dear to me'. This is a further step, and the Gītā closes with the plea, 'well beloved art thou of me . . . for thou art dear to me'. Kṛishṇa had already said that Arjuna is beloved by him, and now he presses even further and says that he is well beloved, or 'positively desired [*iṣṭa*] by him'. Rāmānuja later took this further and spoke of the reciprocity of the love of God and man: 'Just as he who approaches me as his ultimate goal cannot maintain himself in existence without me, so too I cannot maintain myself without him. Thus he is my very soul.'[16]

This is a secret, the mystical secret, of the union of man and God. The Gītā ends with the warning that such teaching is 'never to be spoken to one who is not austere in life, or has no devotion in him, or is not obedient, or speaks ill of me'. Pearls must not be cast before swine. This is a 'supreme secret' for devotees, more secret than the secret.[17]

Union with God had been the aim of all Upanishadic teaching. The Gītā had early considered this, and taught that beyond liberation, beyond becoming Brahman and entering the *nirvāṇa* of Brahman, there is a loving relationship with God. Being liberated man is said to attain to God, and come to him like a pupil going to a teacher. But then by worship he becomes fit to participate in God, 'becomes worthy of my state' and 'attains to my being'. And finally the devotee is said actually to enter into God: 'having known me in truth, he enters at once into me'.[18]

Thus the Gītā goes beyond the mysticism of identity to mysticism of union, in which nevertheless there are loving relationships between man and God. On this foundation the later *bhakti* mystics built: Jayadeva, Tulsīdās, Mīrabāī, Vidyāpati, Chaitanya, and so on, down to Rabīndranāth Tagore in our day, one of the purest and best of all.

It is sometimes thought that the Bible is unmystical, and even that true Christianity is incompatible with the mystical experience and claims. The emphasis on the transcendence of God and man's insignificance, to be found in the Old Testament and certain kinds of Protestantism, is against the mystical aim of union with God. On the other hand this mystical spirit is to be found in the New Testament, in both eastern and western Catholic devotion, in Pietism on the Continent, and in both Methodist and Anglo-Catholic movements in England. It is chiefly in Calvinism that mysticism can hardly flourish, and a reassessment of Protestant mysticism is overdue.

There is, however, still some confusion and uneasiness in Christian circles over mysticism, because of the common fashion for identifying all kinds of Hindu, Buddhist and Christian mysticisms and regarding them all as alike and equal. The indifferentist thinks that all religions are the same. The Christian objects that this takes anything unique or even arresting out of his revelation, and removes any reason for being a Christian, or for that matter a Hindu. The same discrimination must be made, therefore, between different types of mysticism as we made above in considering Hinduism.

If there is any Biblical or Christian mysticism it is certain that it differs from some kinds of Hindu mysticism, while it is akin to other kinds. The Yoga type of mystic who tries to realize the eternal nature of his own soul by his own efforts, and the Upanishadic type who seeks identity with the ground of all things but not with a personal God, have no parallel in the Bible, and little enough in any of the Christian traditions.

The only kind of mysticism that can claim a basis in the Bible and be characteristic of Christianity is the theistic type. This is the mystic who seeks the I-Thou relationship with God. It is not surprising that it is a modern Jewish mystic who has made this clear, Martin Buber in his classic little book *I and Thou*. Here he says quite bluntly, 'God comprises, but is not, the Universe. So too God comprises, but is not, my Self. . . . God does not permit himself to be held.'[19]

A good deal of the Old Testament stresses God's transcendent holiness and man's sin and smallness before him. But other parts give expression to an attitude of ardent devotion that is the beginning, at least, of mystical love. The Shema, the great commandment, which is still regarded by Jews as the essence of the Old Testament, and was chosen by Jesus as the first and great law, begins: 'Shema [hear], Israel, the Lord our God is one Lord; and thou shalt love the Lord thy God with all thy heart, and with all thy soul, and with all thy might.'[20]

Love to God is expressed many times in the Hebrew scriptures; love of his name, his house, the place where his honour dwells, his salvation, commandments, law and testimonies, all these are repeated and dwelt on. Especially is this so in the Psalms, e.g. Psalm 42: 'As the hart pants after the waterbrooks, so pants my soul after thee, O God; my soul thirsts for God, for the living God.' This is not a mere liturgical expression or communal chant, but it breathes a strongly personal spirit. So again in Psalm 63: 'O God, thou art my God, early will I seek thee; my soul thirsts for thee, my flesh longs after thee, in a dry and weary land, where no water is. . . . For thy lovingkindness is better than life.'

It might yet be argued that the Old Testament speaks for society, for the people of Israel, and not in a truly personal and individual sense. The theologian who agrees to this has been overawed by anthropologists or sociologists, who often maintain that religion is a projection of society, or at least that in ancient religions men never met God in solitude. But there are many Biblical examples of men with solitary religious experience, from Moses to Elijah, Jesus and Paul.

There are outstanding Old Testament examples of men in close communion with God. Jeremiah wrestled and debated with God: 'O Lord, thou hast deceived me and I was deceived. . . . And if I say I will not make mention of him, nor speak any more in his name, then there is in my heart as it were a burning fire shut up in my bones, and I am weary with forbearing and I cannot contain.' This is not a completely transcendent God, and Hosea spoke often of the love of God: 'When Israel was a child then I loved him, and called my son out of Egypt. . . . I drew them with cords of a man, with bands of love. . . . My heart is turned within me, my compassions are kindled together.'[21]

The Biblical view of God, and man's relationships with him, are deeply personal. Hence comes the stress on the providence, care, pity, tenderness, compassion and love of God. There is no indifference by God, to good men or evil, to just or unjust; however impartial he may be he is always full of concern for them. So the offences of the wicked provoke him, as the goodness of the righteous pleases him. This may be taken to extremes, but there is never any doubt of the personal relationship, the I-Thou nexus. God never treats man as a thing, an it, and if man treats God in this way it is a grave abuse of fellowship. Although many symbolical expressions were used about God, in a way the prophets were trying to reverse the process of the Gītā, and pass beyond the manifest to the unmanifested.

Even if God were completely transcendent that need not ban mysticism, as the history of Islam shows. R. A. Nicholson, writing of the Ṣūfīs, says, 'The infinite distance between God and man God alone can annihilate; man has no power to bridge the chasm, therefore it is overleaped by a tour de force of the omnipotent Will.... God in a sudden gleam reveals himself as ineffably near. Must not the distinction between subject and object vanish altogether? For here God is all, and there is naught beside him.'[22] So the most completely transcendental doctrine of Islam gave way to mystical union, and even to identity in some Ṣūfīs.

But Christianity through its very nature asserts the revelation of God, his nearness to men, his union yet difference from them. Nicholson argues that the Christian doctrine of the Trinity, 'though it does not affirm the personality *of* God, affirms the existence of personal relations *in* his nature.... It has been found easier in Christianity than elsewhere "to secure what may be called a personal religion without a mystical dissipation of its Object".'[23]

In Christianity the symbol returns, the way of the Manifest surpasses the unmanifest or imperfectly manifest. Of Christ it is said that 'He is the image [εἰκών] of the invisible God, the first-born of all creation.' And again, 'He is the effulgence of his glory, and the very image [χαρακτήρ] of his substance' (ὑπόστασις).[24]

The New Testament teaching of the Incarnation shows God present with man: 'God was in Christ, reconciling the world to himself.' And the purpose of this Incarnation was to dissolve all barriers of ignorance and sin and draw man into union with God. The divine Logos was 'in the world, and the world was made by him, but the world knew him not'. So he 'became flesh and dwelt among us and we beheld his glory'. No man has ever seen or can see the infinite God, but he is revealed to man in 'the Son' who is from the very heart of the Father. And this is not simply revelation of truth or grace, but has the aim of unity with God, 'I in them and thou in me.'[25]

Here the New Testament is closely akin to the devotional mysticism of Hinduism. It has been rightly said that 'the whole mass of Pauline and Johannine teaching is mystical to the core'. Of this theistic mysticism Christians need have no fear, for it is at the very origins and heart of their faith.[26]

This teaching begins in the Synoptic Gospels, with 'Come unto me, all ye that are weary and heavy laden', with 'the kingdom of God is within you', and with the promises, 'I am with you always', and 'where two or three are gathered together in my name, there am I in the midst'. In Matthew the relationship of Jesus to the Father is paralleled by that of the disciples to himself, and this is taken up and extended in the Johannine writings.[27]

The mystical relationship of men to God is one of love and intimate union. 'Abide in me and I in you. . . . Abide in my love.' In the high-priestly prayer of John 17 eternal life is said to be to know God and Christ, but union with God is more than mere knowledge: 'Even as thou, Father, art in me, and I in thee, that they also may be in us . . . that the love wherewith thou lovedst me may be in them, and I in them.'

Paul constantly speaks in such terms: 'That Christ may dwell in your hearts through faith.' This is 'the breadth and length and depth and height . . . to know the love of Christ . . . that you may be filled with all the fulness [πλήρωμα] of God'. And the epistle of Peter speaks of becoming 'partakers of the divine nature' (sharing in the very being of God).[28]

This seems to be coming close to the monistic identification of the soul with God, but it would be a mistake to read this into the Bible. Even if man is akin to God in nature, his soul being the immortal breath of God, yet the fact that the breath can be regarded separately means that there is a distinctive relationship subsisting between man and God.

Biblical and Christian mysticism sees beyond communion to union with God. But this is not identity, becoming God or being dissolved into him. Like Rāmānuja the Christian sees loving relationships with God persisting eternally. The goal of Christian mysticism is not nothingness or absorption, but union with God and the beatific vision.

References

1. Ṛig Veda 3, 68; 5, 85; 3, 62, 10.
2. *Hindu Mysticism*, p. 42.
3. ib. p. 80.
4. ib. p. 55.
5. Taittirīya Upanishad 1, 4; Śvetāśvatara 6, 18.
6. Śvet. 6, 7; 6, 1; 6, 23.
7. Ṛig Veda 10, 125, 5; Kaṭha 2, 20 f.; Śvet. 3, 20.
8. Bhagavad Gītā 9, 28; 18, 54.
9. ib. 11, 9.
10. ib. 12, 5. Quoted by S. Radhakrishnan, *The Bhagavadgītā*, p. 293.
11. Gītā 9, 11; 9, 15; 17, 3.
12. Quoted in *Hindu and Muslim Mysticism*, p. 195.
13. Gītā 11, 44.
14. ib. 9, 29. Radhakrishnan, p. 250.
15. Gītā 10, 11; 12, 7.
16. ib. 12, 14 ff.; 18, 64 f. See *Hindu and Muslim Mysticism*, pp. 76, 197.
17. Gītā 18, 67.
18. ib. 9, 28; 10, 10; 13, 18; 14, 19; 18, 55.
19. *I and Thou*, p. 95.
20. Deuteronomy 6, 4–5.
21. Jeremiah 20, 7–12; Hosea 11, 1–7; 14, 4 f.
22. *The Idea of Personality in Ṣūfism*, p. 13.
23. ib. p. 11.
24. Colossians 1, 15; Hebrews 1, 3.
25. 2 Cor. 5, 19; John 1, 10; 1, 18; 17, 23.
26. *At Sundry Times*, p. 172.
27. Matthew 11, 28; Luke 17, 21; Matt. 28, 20; 18, 20
28. Eph. 3, 17 f.; 2 Peter 1, 4 (*New English Bible*).

Chapter 9

CONDUCT AND SUFFERING

In the early Bṛihad-āraṇyaka Upanishad we read that conduct determines destiny, as we act so do we become. 'According as one acts, according as one behaves, so does he become. The doer of good becomes good. The doer of evil becomes evil. One becomes virtuous by virtuous action, bad by bad action. . . . As is his desire, so is his will; as is his will, so is his action [*karma*].'[1]

The concept of *karma* (action, deeds, from a root *kṛi*, to do or make) is logical and scientific. It is the result of observing cause and effect, of order or the working of law in the world.

In the hymns of the Ṛig Veda the term *ṛita* was used to indicate the cosmic order on which human order depends, both moral and social. *Ṛita* was first of all the regular order of nature, the succession of the seasons and of sun and moon, and in sacrifice for them Agni, the divine fire, was the guardian of *ṛita* in the ritual sense. But Varuṇa, the most lofty deity of the Ṛig Veda, was the guardian of *ṛita* in a moral sense. 'Varuṇa, true to holy law, sits among his people. Most wise, he sits to govern all.' He sees all things, dispenses justice and hears men's cries. His is not a harsh legalism, however, for every prayer to Varuṇa has a plea for forgiveness.

Karma, in the Upanishads, shows the causation of things, their origins and effects, and it demonstrates morality. Actions generate a kind of energy, invisible and unique, and this works upon the soul and determines its present course and future destiny. So it is asked, 'When a man dies what does not leave him?' And the answer was *karma*, and what was praised was *karma*. One becomes good by good action (*karma*), and evil by evil action.[2]

Karma, as we saw earlier, effects transmigration, and brings man down again to an embodied existence; those whose conduct has been pleasant will have a pleasant rebirth, but those whose conduct stinks will enter a stinking birth.[3]

Conduct, then, has an abiding effect. Actions follow the soul from one life to another, identifying it without hesitation, 'as the calf finds its mother in a herd of many cows'.

This is the Hindu solution of the problems of man's lot in life, the inequalities of station, and the tragedy of suffering. It is sometimes said that Hinduism neglects this problem, and it does appear that there was much less concern and speculation over it than in some other religions. But part of the reason, at least, is that the solution to the problem seemed ready made and watertight. What you are now, however lowly and unhappy, is the result of your own actions in a previous existence. You have nobody else to blame, neither man nor God. Indeed, this is the working of implacable justice, and it would be unjust to change it in favour of a temporary alleviation of pain, even supposing that could be done. But the teaching is not necessarily fatalistic, you can improve your lot. *Karma* will work itself out, and you can accumulate good *karma* that will ensure a happier lot in the next round of rebirth.

It is said also that the teaching of *karma* is pessimistic, but the Upanishads are not so. While there are many statements about the unsatisfactoriness of this life compared with eternity, yet the importance of good action and knowledge is stressed. The Upanishads do not urge the Buddhist view of the misery of existence, although they do share in the search for liberation from the constant round of transmigration.

Nor do the Upanishads teach complete determinism. This was the solution adopted by the sect of the Ājīvikas, contemporary with the Buddhists and the Jains. The Ājīvikas opposed the notion that a man can work out his own salvation, for their fundamental principle was the supremacy of Fate (*niyati*). Fate was the motive power of the universe and sole agent of all change. Good and bad were all subject to one ruling principle: 'just as a ball of thread when thrown will unwind to its full length, so fool and wise alike will take their course and make an end of sorrow'. Rather inconsistently *karma* was still included in the scheme, but it had no real moral force and was unaffected by good or evil living. The path of transmigration was set out rigidly, the same for every soul, which had to pass through the same course over a period of more than eight million great ages.[4]

This deadly determinism was not accepted by Hindus, Buddhists or Jains. But the Hindu teaching hardly approached the problem systematically. The relationship between *karma* and human liberty, and the problems and contradictions that might arise there, were barely touched on. More important were the different kinds of *karma*, and the relationship between *karma* and the divine power in the world.

The Upanishads speak of good *karma* and inferior *karma* (inferior because lacking in knowledge), and of past *karma* which still impels man to perform actions in this present life. Work does not make a Brahmin, but *karma* accumulated in the previous embodiment, begun in the present, or to commence in the future, these impel men to perform work.[5]

Later writers distinguished between the seeds of *karma* sown by past actions which have not yet begun to grow, then *karma* of the past life which was already germinating, and finally *karma* which would grow up in this present life because of ignorance. The enlightened sage would destroy latent *karma* and not acquire new *karma*, while that which had begun to germinate would continue as long as he remained in this embodied existence.

The completely enlightened sage was no longer really active. At least he was not active in heart, knowing that the phenomenal world is illusion, and gazing at its passing show like a man watching a magical performance. So complete indifference to all activity, and even to good and evil, must be reached if one is to be freed from the entanglements of transmigration.

Heinrich Zimmer, the great Indologist, said that 'a basic fact generally disregarded by those who "go in" for Indian wisdom is this one of the total rejection of every last value of humanity. . . .

Perfect non-activity, in thought, speech, and deed, is possible only when one has become dead to *every* concern of life.... The sublime and gentle final fetter, virtue, is thus itself something to be severed.... Humanity and its problems ... can be of no interest to one who has literally died to time.'[6]

However, there are different paths and in the Bhagavad Gītā the problems of compassion, work or no work, detachment and devotion, are raised and treated in some detail.

One problem that does emerge from the teaching of *karma* is an apparently impersonal and legalistic attitude to life and conduct. *Karma* works (like *ṛita*) as a cosmic law, seemingly regardless of God or the divine, and so there would appear to be little room for a religious attitude, or at least it would not make much difference whether there is one or not. And the possibility of repentance and forgiveness seems to be ruled out, or at least irrelevant.

Yet in the Ṛig Vedic hymns there were appeals to Varuṇa for forgiveness. 'Varuṇa, hear this cry of mine, be gracious to us this day; longing for help I cry to thee ... to gain thy mercy we bind thy heart with hymns.' And again, 'If we have sinned against the man who loves us ... O Varuṇa, remove the trespass from us.... Let us be thine own beloved.'[7] Here are the notes of theistic religion, polytheistic perhaps, but personal and giving the hope of pardon. The will of God controls the world order and can grant forgiveness.

It is sometimes said, especially by Buddhists, that the act of repentance and the granting of pardon are immoral, or even impossible. They demand an alteration of the laws of nature which is strictly impossible. But this is to apply the laws of the external world to the very different realm of personal relationships. It is true that cause and effects, crime and punishment, are fixed and unalterable between things or in abstract codes. But they are not immutable between persons. Persons can and do break their own laws, they can forgive or refuse to do so. And it makes all the difference in the world to a religion if it is taken impersonally (in an I-it relationship), as in early Buddhism where the law is inflexible; or whether the religion is taken personally (I-Thou), as in the Semitic religions, the early Vedas, the Gītā, and Mahāyāna Buddhism, where penitence and pardon both feature.

The Upanishads hold a mediating place between the theism of the Ṛig Vedic hymns and the impersonal system of early Buddhism. But they are directed by their constant view of the supremacy of the divine, Brahman-ātman. It is because of his essentially divine nature that man is able to work out his *karma* and finally to rid himself of it. Were it not so he would be imprisoned without hope in the determinism of the Ājīvikas, where no divine power could hold sway.

The impersonal and legalistic attitude may be modified also in the notion of rewards and punishments. A good birth is the reward of past good behaviour, and an evil life is the punishment for bad actions. This does act as a spur to future action, and while finally one should act without any eye on the future, yet human nature is such that the results of action are weighed and valued. So the Laws of Manu admit that 'to act solely from a desire for rewards is not laudable, yet exemption from that desire is not found in this world'. Indeed they say that study of the Vedas and obedience to their commands are based on hope of rewards.[8]

Rewards and punishments certainly play a part as motives of conduct in some of the earlier texts and moral treatises, but in later works, and notably in the Gītā, the importance of acting without attachment to rewards is strongly emphasized.

In the Bhagavad Gītā the way of works (*karma-yoga*) is shown to be important and valid. In answer to Arjuna's query about fighting his kinsmen, he is told to fight because that is his caste duty: 'there is no greater good for a warrior than a battle enjoined by duty'. Everyone has duties appropriate to the state of life in which he finds himself. If the action is disagreeable, it must still be done. There is no escape by inaction, for in fact 'nobody can remain for a moment without acting'. So one must do the allotted work, since action is better than inaction and freedom is not attained by abstention from work. The great man should give an example of work to lesser beings. Indeed the Lord himself is at work, ever sustaining the universe; 'if I should cease to work these worlds would fall in ruin'. (Compare the Gospel statement, 'My Father has never yet ceased his work, and I am working too.'[9])

However, the Gītā solves the problem of disagreeable and repugnant action, as well as the question of how to avoid the contamination of *karma*, by teaching the way of non-attachment. Hope of reward, the fruit of action, must be given up completely. Duty should be done with indifference, renouncing all results. He who gives up the fruit of action is the true renouncer. And, finally, the supreme state which transcends all work is attained by him whose understanding is unattached, who has subdued his self, and from whom all desire has fled.[10]

Dasgupta comments on this: 'The great solution of the Gita is the compromise it advances between the worldly life of allotted duties and the hermit life of absolute renouncement, and between a life of lawful and proper enjoyment and the absolute extinction of desires. The program that it proposes is, on the one hand, that we purify our minds, purging them of all attachments and passions by dedicating all the fruits of our actions to God; and yet, on the other hand, that we continue to perform all the duties belonging to our particular caste or stage of life.'[11]

So far the teaching of the Gītā is akin to that of Buddhism, which was doubtless well advanced at the time when the Gītā was composed. The Buddha also taught the importance of right action, right speech, and right livelihood. The destruction of *karma* through abnegation would finally bring about the cessation of rebirth and the attainment of *nirvāṇa*. The last words attributed to the Buddha were 'exert yourselves in wakefulness'. (Dr. E. Conze says that Protestant utilitarian administrators in Ceylon and Burma seized on this verse as characteristic of a non-supernatural religion; but it is absent from other versions which say simply, 'doomed to extinction are all composite things'.[12])

But religion is more than ethics, and conduct on its side seems to need a warmer motive than just self-help. Religion is concerned with personal relationships, and so it is above the sphere of natural law. Buddhism itself in the Mahāyāna version developed from 'an original atheism into a constellation of theistic systems'.[13]

And even Theravāda (Hīnayāna) Buddhism has its innumerable shrines and Buddha images before which the faithful bow in adoration.

We have seen that in the Upanishads theism reappears beside monism. The suggestion is made that the vision of God brings works to an end. 'The knot of the heart is cut, all doubts are dispelled, and one's deeds [*karma*] cease, when he is seen.' And again, 'he is to be obtained only by the one whom he chooses, to such a one that Soul reveals his own person'.[14]

And in the Gītā the way of faith and devotion is taught as the most perfect yoga of all. The grace of God works with man to bring him to the eternal abode. Man must do all the necessary actions, but by taking refuge in the Lord he will reach the goal. Actions must, in fact, be surrendered to God, and thought constantly fixed on him, then by his grace all difficulties will be overcome.[15] *Karma-yoga* is a valid path but *bhakti-yoga* is the best.

Nature will compel you to work, even against your will; but if you fly to God with all your being you will obtain eternal peace by his grace. So the solution of the Gītā to the problem of action, the impulses of nature, and duty to be done in this world, is this deeply religious answer of the grace of God and the devotion of man.

In contrast to the impersonal, natural, almost scientific teaching of the Upanishads upon conduct and its karmic results in suffering or deliverance, the Biblical starting-point is the opposite one of personal relationships. However, during their history the Hebrews did not always maintain this level.

God was thought of as a person, never as a neuter force, and so his dealings with men were always personal like those between human beings. At its lower levels the notion of a jealous or angry God (so offensive to modern taste, though often found also in popular Hinduism) was the expression of this belief in the personal concern of God for every aspect of life. God could not be detached and untouched by man's misdoings. On a higher plane men saw that their deeds were not merely social offences but sins against God; 'Against thee, thee only, have I sinned.'[16]

The emphasis upon sin in the Bible, as an offence against God, contrasts with its comparative absence in other religions, or else their view of sin as ritual impurity. The importance of harmony with God, with his revealed will, brought the accompaniment of remorse and penitence when that harmony was broken.

Although it was God who was said to visit 'the iniquity of the fathers upon the children, to the third and fourth generation', yet the idea of inherited guilt or punishment has an automatic and legalistic ring about it. This is what Ezekiel had in mind later when he combated the notion of inherited guilt (and by analogy of original sin), in one of his most famous chapters. You must no longer use this proverb, 'the fathers have eaten sour grapes, and the children's teeth are set on edge'. Ezekiel opposes this belief in a son bearing his father's iniquity, by putting it back firmly into the realm of personal relationship with God. 'Behold all souls are mine, as the soul of the father, so also the soul of the son is mine. . . . The son shall not bear the iniquity of the father. . . . For I have no pleasure in the death of him that dies. . . . He that has walked in my statutes . . . he is just, he shall surely live.' And again, 'if the wicked turns from his sins . . . he shall surely live'.[17]

In the New Testament the struggle of Jesus with the Pharisees, and later of Paul with the Law, which may now seem to be remote or dry, was precisely this issue of legalism; whether it was an impersonal law or a personal relationship which governed men's actions and their attitude to God.

It is a common error to suppose that the Gospels were basically or originally moral treatises, and that Jesus was primarily an ethical teacher. The Sermon on the Mount, so often regarded as the essence of his teaching, is an amalgam of many sayings from different periods. It is an ethical and religious catechism, compiled for the use of Christian converts. Almost every verse presupposes a larger original context; e.g. the verse about forgiving others presupposes the parable of the unmerciful servant.[18]

* The concern of Jesus was to bring men into a new relationship with God, all men, including the outcast. Unlike most of the world's great teachers Jesus sought his audience not simply among

the naturally pious, or those interested in religious questions, but among the rough fishermen, the shady tax collectors, the political traitors and the prostitutes. All these were sought out and offered a new relationship with God, from which good conduct would then flow.

Jesus said very little about sin; but forgiveness and healing, the deliverance of soul and body from bondage, were prominent in his message. To the paralytic he brought new life, saying first 'your sins are forgiven'. In the case of the man born blind the interesting question of whether he or his parents sinned was brushed aside, but the healing grace of God was shown. Careless of his own defilement Jesus went to eat with outcasts from respectable Jewish society, like Levi, Zacchaeus, and the Samaritans. But the forgiveness that he brought was not immoral, nor did it dispense with the necessity for a changed life and restitution for past evil deeds. So Zacchaeus declared that he would restore fourfold to anyone he had wronged.[19]

The Pharisaic effort was too often legalistic, directed towards a scrupulous observance of a multitude of laws and traditions for their own sake. They strained at the gnat of slight impurity, and swallowed the camel of injustice, leaving undone 'the weightier matters of the law, justice, mercy and faith'. So they kept the penitent away from God by their own self-righteousness. Jesus remarked sarcastically that he had not come to call the righteous but sinners, and demanded that his followers should exceed the righteousness of the Pharisees—in mercy. God preferred mercy to sacrifice.

Professor T. E. Jessop has pointed out that ethical teachings were only incidental to the teaching of Jesus. They grew out of the events of religious salvation. But circumstances alter cases. Jesus did not set up a new and even harder Mosaic law, and laid down no inflexible principles. It is just as much a mistake to apply the words of Jesus rigidly as it was for the Pharisee so to treat the law.[20]

Paul more laboriously, but with sure insight, saw that legalism cannot produce the right relationship with God, and so the right religious norm of conduct. The law, he said, gives only the knowledge of sin. There is no salvation by *karma-yoga*, so to speak. 'For the good that I would I do not, but the evil that I would not, that I do. . . . Who will deliver me from the body of this death?' The answer is in *bhakti-yoga*, faith in grace: 'I thank God through Jesus Christ.'[21]

It is well known that James in his epistle seems to combat the stress that Paul laid on faith. 'Faith, if it has not works, is dead.' But this is the other side of the same argument. There is no suggestion that faith is not needed: 'I by my works will show thee my faith.' The real enemy is superficial believing, the attitude of the man who imagines that he is above others and freed from any obligation to them.[22]

Paul also speaks of the law of cause and effect: 'whatsoever a man sows that also shall he reap'. But this is no natural law apart from God, for the Hebrew mind could never agree to any abstract principle prior to or independent of God. And this very law of cause and effect is transmuted in that 'he that sows to the Spirit shall of the Spirit reap eternal life'. The Christian is no longer under the law but under the Spirit, and produces the fruits of the Spirit which include both peace and kindness.[23]

The importance of grace and personal relationships in Biblical religion affects all its moral teachings and guidance on conduct. The motive of action is love, not rewards; to deny oneself and save others. The highest ideal is not detachment, but service to others, even at the cost of losing oneself.[24]

It is strange that while the Upanishads are generally given to speculation, and the Bible is in the main didactic, this position should be reversed where the problem of suffering is concerned. The doctrine of *karma* provided an answer for Indian minds to the gross inequalities of life, its diseases, accidents, tragedies, and death itself. All would be worked out in future embodiments, through that inexorable law of *karma*. This answer appeared to satisfy not only Hindus, but also Buddhists and Jains.

Such an answer was impossible to the Hebrews, because it was impersonal. If suffering came it was from God. So the suffering of the wicked was explicable, but that of the righteous was an affront to their faith. Conduct should be rewarded justly; the punishment should fit the crime, and the reward the virtue. If God was just, as he must be, then a serious moral and religious problem arose if injustice appeared and the innocent suffered. So they wrestled with this problem as Hindus did not, because it touched the foundations of their personal religion.

So Habakkuk asked God, 'Wherefore lookest thou upon them that deal treacherously, and holdest thy peace when the wicked swallows up the man that is more righteous than he?' Jeremiah demanded to know, 'wherefore does the way of the wicked prosper?' Psalm 73 wondered at the prosperity of the wicked, but foresaw a violent end for them. With less easy optimism Psalm 77 asked if God had forgotten to be gracious, but decided that this question was human infirmity and one must remember God's goodness in the past.[25]

But the bitter question of the suffering of the righteous is treated at great length and with discrimination in the book of Job. It is said that there are half a dozen answers to the problem given in this book, none of them entirely satisfactory though some are very near the truth. The orthodox answer is given by Job's 'comforters', that all suffering is the result of sin (or *karma*), hidden if not open; but this is rejected throughout the book. The prose prologue sees the troubles of the just as a trial of faith sent by God, and the epilogue shows that this is for a time only, everything will come right in the end. There is a slight suggestion in the middle of the book that if things do not come right in this life they will in the next, 'without my flesh I shall see God'. But the text here is corrupt and this cannot be strongly argued though it is often adopted by Christians.

The main burden of the verse drama of Job is that man cannot hope to fathom the divine purposes, only God knows. 'Shall he that cavilleth contend with the Almighty?' This is true, though not very consoling. It means that responsibility is put upon God for all that happens, and the ultimate answer of Job is that the suffering of the just is a mystery.[26]

There is a further answer to the problem of suffering given in the Old Testament, in Second Isaiah. This is that the suffering of the righteous is on behalf of others: 'he was wounded for our transgressions . . . and with his stripes we are healed'. This is vicarious suffering, expressive of the unity of mankind, whereby the innocent suffer for the guilty. Applied first to the suffering nation of Israel, this teaching is taken up in the New Testament and applied to Christ. He 'suffered for sins once, the just for the unjust, that he might bring us to God'. Suffering is still a mystery, but it is not without purpose. Through his humanity the divine Christ bears the sins of the world, so that men might be reconciled to God and restored to their proper relationship with him. By identification with Christ other men may share in redemptive suffering and 'fill up that which is lacking of the afflictions of Christ'.[27]

References

1. Bṛihad-āraṇyaka Upanishad 4, 4, 5.
2. Ṛig Veda 1, 25, 10; Bṛih. 3, 2, 13.
3. Chāndogya 5, 10, 7.
4. A. L. Basham, *History and Doctrines of the Ājīvikas* (Luzac, 1951), pp. 224 f.
5. Vajrasūchika Upanishad 7.
6. *Philosophies of India*, pp. 231 f.
7. Ṛig Veda 1, 25, 19; 5, 85, 7.
8. Manu 2, 2.
9. Bhagavad Gītā 2, 31; 3, 5; 3, 24. John 5, 17 (*New English Bible*).
10. Gītā 18, 49.
11. *Hindu Mysticism*, p. 117.
12. 'Recent Progress in Buddhist Studies', in *The Middle Way*, July 1959.
13. *At Sundry Times*, p. 104.
14. Muṇḍaka 2, 2, 8; 3, 2, 3; Kaṭha 2, 23.
15. Gītā 18, 56 ff.
16. Psalm 51, 4.
17. Ezekiel 18.
18. Matthew 6, 14; 18, 21 ff.
19. Mark 2, 5; Luke 19, 8.
20. *Law and Love* (Epworth, 1948), pp. 1 ff.

21. Romans 7, 19–25.
22. James 2, 17–18.
23. Galatians 6, 7 f.
24. Mark 8, 35; 15, 31.
25. Habakkuk 1, 13; Jeremiah 12, 1.
26. Job 19, 26 (R.S.V.); 40, 2.
27. Isaiah 53, 5; 1 Peter 3, 18; John 1, 29; Col. 1, 24.

Chapter 10

RELIGION AND SOCIETY

In the foregoing chapters similarities and differences have been noted between Indian and Hebrew thought. It often seems that speculation is on the Hindu side, while the Bible is content with dogmatic assertion, or has little reasoned teaching on the subject in hand, for example the immortality of the soul in the Old Testament. A notable exception is the problem of suffering. But when we come to the role played by religion in society, and its social and moral teaching, the position is changed. Here the Bible is the great teacher of social ethics, and the Upanishads have little to say about them.

It must be said that the Upanishads are treatises and speculations about religious philosophy, and not systems of ethics. They are concerned with interpreting the universe, the world soul and the human soul, and they hardly go beyond this to tackle the problems of moral and social conduct. So Keith says, 'In comparison with the intellectual activity of the Brahmans the ethical content of the Upaniṣads must be said to be negligible and valueless. . . . There are, here and there, moral maxims enunciated, but these are of no consequence and rise in no way above popular morality. On the contrary . . . the possession of knowledge makes a man independent of all morality.'[1]

This may seem a harsh judgement but Dasgupta confirms not only that the enlightened man is above morality, but that he becomes indifferent to other people. One who gave himself wholly to the pursuit of liberation (*moksha*) could have little time for concern about other people. 'No one who sought the absolute freedom of his own self, or the extinction of his whole personality like the extinguishing of a flame, and who sought the cessation of his own rebirths and sorrow as the only goal and ambition to be realized, could have much scope for any active manifestation of universal friendship. . . . Tales of self-sacrifice from the motive of universal friendship are very rare, and they do not seem to fit in with the Hindu ideal of personal and individual liberation.'[2] Some yogis are like the lonely rhinoceros who lives apart, is not instructed by anyone, and does not teach others to impart his knowledge to them. Others are gurus who have groups of pupils.

There are a few references to moral example. The Taittirīya Upanishad instructs pupils to speak the truth, practise virtue (*dharma*), and treat mother and father, teacher and guest, as gods. One should take the model of Brahmins who are apt, devoted and lovers of virtue.[3] Later Hinduism took the noble lives of Rāma and Sītā as patterns of heroic and chaste life, and there has been a constant veneration of heroes and holy men, down to Mahātmā Gāndhi and others today.

Seeking after pleasure is condemned. The demon Virochana concluded that one should be happy here on earth and the body served, and so through clothes and adornments yonder world would be gained. This hedonism is rejected as the doctrine of demons. So the young Nachiketas in the House of Death refused the offer of the greatest earthly pleasures, preferring to know the secret of immortality.[4]

So far as concern for others is taught in the Upanishads, it is in relation to the world-soul; this is said repeatedly. 'Not for love of the husband is a husband dear, but for love of the soul [*ātman*] a husband is dear. Not for love of the wife is a wife dear, but for love of the soul a wife is dear.' This is against hedonism, of course; it teaches that people and things are not valuable for the pleasure they give, but rather that they are valuable only as phases of the world-soul. In love for others we find the larger soul. Hume comments on this, 'So far as it contains ethical theory, this represents the high-water mark in the Upanishads. The practical ethics are certainly not as high.'[5]

In the Bhagavad Gītā the opening complaint of Arjuna is a real concern for other people. 'He was overcome with great compassion, and uttered this in sadness . . . I do not long for victory. . . . Of what use is dominion to us? . . . I could not wish to kill these people, even though they were to kill me. . . . It is not right to slay our kinsmen.'[6]

This is a humane plea, based on compassion, recognizing the folly of warfare and the cruelty of killing other people. But Radhakrishnan's comment is that Arjuna 'is stressing the physical pain and the material discomfort which warfare involves. The main end of life is not the pursuit of material happiness. . . . He has yet to realize that wives and children, teachers and kinsmen, are dear not for their own sake but for the sake of the Self.'[7] This is the classical answer, but it does not appear to reach the heart of the problem of compassion, which sees foes as people, valuable in their own right.

The two answers given by the Gītā itself to Arjuna's problem are those of duty and reality beyond delusion. The duty is to fulfil one's caste obligation whatever it may be: 'There is no greater good for a Kshatriya than a battle enjoined by duty.' It is right to fight, not only in self-defence but under orders and in accordance with one's rank.[8]

The teaching of reality beyond illusion is that the warrior cannot kill the soul, death cannot destroy that which never dies. 'If the slayer thinks to slay, if the slain thinks himself slain, both of these do not understand. He does not slay, nor is he slain.' The true self is imperishable, and so it does not matter what happens to the body. This seems cold comfort, or stern morality, and there is some deviation from it in the later ideal of harmlessness (*ahiṁsā*). Once again the Gītā contains varying points of view.[9]

The ideal given in the Gītā is consistent with the main trend of Upanishadic teaching, of 'One unconcerned . . . who stands apart . . . the same to friends and foes.' But it goes beyond this. The Upanishads regard moral distinctions and common activities as inapplicable to the man who has metaphysical knowledge. But the Gītā explains that work must be done, though without attachment. Yet the yogi should have his understanding unattached everywhere, subdue his self, expel desire. He should dwell in solitude, eat little, control body and mind, neither grieve nor desire, and regard all beings as alike. He is unconcerned, thinking pleasure and pain alike, 'the same in honour and dishonour, and the same to friends and foes'.[10]

Such a devotee not only behaves alike to friends and enemies, but he has also 'renounced good and evil'. This is startling to those who have been brought up in the Semitic religions. But Radhakrishnan explains it to mean that the struggle of goodness with its opposite has ceased and, having become absolute, 'it ceases to be goodness and goes beyond all ethical compulsion'. Certainly the true yogi is said to be one who has 'no ill-will to any being, who is friendly and compassionate, without a thought of me or mine, even-minded in pleasure and pain, longsuffering'.[11]

There was scope here for development of compassion on the Buddhist model, though passively rather than actively. Dasgupta says again: 'The altruistic ideal can therefore at best be merely a disposition, and can manifest itself merely in a negative way, e.g. in non-injury to any being. But a person who holds such an individualistic notion of salvation cannot, in his scheme of life, have any leisure or opportunity for the doing of active good to others.'[12]

The moral and social teachings of Hinduism are rather set out in the Dharmaśāstras or Dharmasūtras, attributed to semi-mythical figures like Manu, and embodying religious and social teachings which grew up over the centuries. *Dharma* in this sense means the duty and rights of men in an ideal society, and so the moral law.

The Laws of Manu give rules of life for the three higher castes, the twice-born: Brahmins, rulers and warriors, and merchants or farmers. This is particularly civil and criminal law and there is little general morality. Caste men are told to honour their relatives, both male and female. A householder should every day 'place on the ground some food for dogs, outcastes and sick'—thus daily honouring all beings. Kings are told to administer justice to everyone, for justice is preserved by justice. Kings must also zealously provide food for all created beings. Ascetics are exhorted to 'patiently bear hard words . . . against an angry man let him not in return show anger, let him bless when he is cursed'. In similar vein the epic Mahābhārata exhorts to 'conquer the anger of others by non-anger; conquer evil-doers by saintliness; conquer the miser by gifts; conquer falsehood by truth'.[13]

The summary of the law for the four castes is given by Manu as 'abstention from injury, veracity, abstention from unlawfully appropriating the goods of others, purity, and control of the organs'. These are the most positive and general commands. There are many others more negative and particular to the upper castes; they do not apply to women, to the lower castes and to out-castes.[14]

The caste system was a social organization of great complexity and rigidity. Its origins seem to have been the Aryan conquest of the older Indian populations, and their pride in a lighter-coloured skin (*varṇa*, colour or caste). Already in the Ṛig Vedic hymns the four main castes were said to come from the body of the primeval man, and this is repeated in the Upanishads. In the Laws of Manu we read that 'in order to protect this universe he, the most resplendent one, assigned separate duties and occupations to those who sprang from his mouth, arms, thighs and feet'. The three upper castes were honoured, especially the Brahmin whose very birth 'is an incarnation of the sacred law'; everything in the world is his property and other mortals exist through his benevolence. The duty of a man of the fourth once-born caste was 'to serve meekly these other three castes', and his very name should 'express something contemptible'.[15]

The extent to which these laws and traditions were applied differed considerably from age to age. Women and Śūdras, though debarred from studying the Vedas and from many rituals, yet were often devout followers of the popular devotional cults, built temples and composed hymns.

The four stages of the life of a caste Hindu expressed certain social duties. After initiation (being born again) he entered the life of a student of sacred knowledge under a teacher. That ended he became a householder, with the duty of marrying and bringing up children. Only after this should he enter the two final stages of hermit and ascetic. Clearly the life of the householder was of most importance socially. Though there was the strong trend of teaching towards renunciation, yet the role of the family man was regarded as essential. Only occasionally do enlightened men declare 'we have no need of offspring'. To marry and produce children and replenish the earth was a fundamental duty, and no less important in tropical India with its many diseases and high mortality than in Palestine and other parts of the earth. So there are detailed rules for the life of a householder, his marriage, religious duties, support of other creatures. If he is a Brahmin, there are many ritual cares, for an outcaste must not even look at him while he is eating. The Brahmin may engage in certain occupations, provided that they do not impede the study of the Vedas or cause pain to other beings.

The occupations to be followed, and the care to avoid taking life, lead on to the teaching of *ahiṁsā* (from a root *han*, to kill), which is non-killing, non-violence, harmlessness. In the Laws of Manu it is said that a twice-born man 'does not seek to cause the sufferings of bonds and death to living creatures, but desires the good of all beings', and so obtains endless bliss. Because of this it recommends restriction of the occupations in which a man of the higher castes might engage. 'A Brahmin or Kshatriya . . . shall carefully avoid agriculture, which causes injury to many beings. . . . For the wooden implement with an iron point injures the earth and life in the earth.'[16]

This doctrine of *ahiṁsā* was especially the teaching of the Jains, who flourished during Upanishadic times. *Ahiṁsā* was based on the belief in the unity of all life, human, animal, plant and even atoms of matter. Taking life even by accident brought darkness to the soul and delayed it in the upward march to *nirvāṇa*. Beasts of prey have very dark souls; so have soldiers, butchers and hunters. In consequence the Jains are strict vegetarians, and many Hindus are also though some will eat meat if they have not killed the animal themselves. It may be imagined what they thought of imperial rulers who claimed to have a superior culture, and spent much of their time hunting, shooting and fishing.

The Jains of course forbade occupations to their followers that would involve taking life, not only hunting and butchery, but also agriculture, lest in digging the ground some animal or insect life be taken. To this day Jain monks brush the road before them in order to avoid treading on insects, and wear white cloths before their mouths to keep insects out. Self-excluded from agriculture the Jains turned to trade and, like the Jews who were prohibited many occupations in Europe, in time they flourished and are often very wealthy.

They did the right thing for the wrong reason!

But somebody must work, for mankind lives off the land, and the Hindu documents recognize this. So the third caste, the Vaiśya, is the mercantile and farming caste. Even a Brahmin may engage in agriculture if he is poor, says Manu, but if he has a Vaiśya to support him then he must avoid farming.

The Gītā speaks of *ahiṁsā* incidentally, as one of the virtues of the religious: 'Purity, uprightness, continence and non-violence, are the penance of the body.' And again, 'non-violence, truth, freedom from anger, renunciation, tranquillity, aversion to fault-finding, compassion to living beings', and so on, these are 'the endowments of him who is born with the divine nature'.[17] This reads almost like St. Paul's list of the fruits of the Spirit, with a characteristically different bias.

The importance of non-injury was to avoid defilement, to preserve one's own tranquillity, and by not taking life to remove one barrier to spiritual progress. Fundamentally negative and self-regarding, it could lead to active compassion. Selfishness and exclusive interest in one's own salvation are sins of the spirit to which all religious people are liable. But active concern with the needs of others is also an outcome of religion, and this was particularly so in Buddhism. Though not always strictly vegetarian, the Buddhist preoccupation with suffering easily took over the ideal of non-violence and proceeded from there to active compassion. The great Indian Buddhist emperor Aśoka (250 B.C.) is renowned for his renunciation of war, prohibition of animal sacrifice and animal foods, building of hospitals for men and animals, digging wells, building rest-houses and planting shade-trees.

It was Mahāyāna Buddhism which held out with such emphasis the ideal of the Bodhisattva who, having attained enlightenment, deferred his own *nirvāṇa* until all other beings were saved. The Indian Buddhist Śānti-deva wrote a great devotional classic in which he tried to surrender his own joy and righteousness, that he might become the servant of the poor and enable all beings to win to their journey's end.[18]

In Hinduism the doctrine of non-violence remained latent until Mahātmā Gāndhi took it up and turned it with such effect to his political and religious ends. Taking over *ahiṁsā* from Jainism, and combining it with the peaceful teaching of the Sermon on the Mount and its interpretation by Tolstoy, Gāndhi successfully defied imperial rule by means of non-warfare. As Zimmer said, this was a 'wizard-priest battle', waged not according to the military textbooks but in the power of Brahman.

His battle done, the abiding significance of Gāndhi's work is to be seen in the awakened social conscience of Hinduism, and also in the Rāmakṛishṇa Mission and in the work of a new kind of holy man like Vinobā Bhāve. The traditional ideal of the yogi working out his own salvation in solitariness and self-concern is challenged in the cause of social justice, freedom for the outcaste, and large schemes to alleviate the lot of the poor. But there are many holy men who keep to the old pattern, and some who openly regret the change of direction.[19]

In these final words on Hindu teaching and practice we have strayed somewhat from simple exposition of the Upanishads and the Gītā. But the ancient *dharma* (law, virtue, righteousness, religion) of the Vedas is claimed by modern Hindus as eternal (*sanātana dharma*). Great developments and changes may be made in religious and social systems; but the ancient scriptures retain their authority for governing the spiritual aspirations of India.

. . . .

In the teaching of the Bible religion is constantly related to ethics. Deviations from this ideal are severely criticized, and the tendency to formalism in ritual is attacked if it hides the moral demands of God. With its strongly personal view of God, his law is held to be binding on men to the fullest degree and to extend not only to individual actions but to the widest social justice.

The height of Old Testament teaching is characterized as 'ethical monotheism', and this was largely the work of the writing prophets of the eighth and seventh centuries B.C. So Amos, denouncing the enclosure systems of the new capitalism of his day, attacked the robbers of the poor who 'have sold the righteous for silver and the needy for a pair of shoes'.

A passion for social justice pierced through the covering of formal religion with which men tried to hide their misdeeds. God, says Amos, does not want such religion: 'I hate, I despise your feasts. . . . But let justice roll down as waters, and righteousness as a mighty stream.'[20]

This was taken up again by his contemporary Hosea who said for God, 'I want mercy and not sacrifice', and even more radically a little later by Isaiah, 'When you pray I will not listen.' The true sacrifice is justice: 'Seek justice, relieve the oppressed, judge the fatherless, plead for the widow.' And Micah set out the ideal, 'What does the Lord require of thee, but to do justly, and to love mercy, and to walk humbly with thy God?'[21]

The prophets championed the rights of the poor, of widows cheated of their living and orphans defrauded of their inheritance by the rich and powerful. The murder of Naboth, at the instigation of Jezebel to gain his vineyard for Ahab, had been violently condemned by Elijah and stood as an example for all time.

The Bible is concerned with people, with their personality and rights. This included slaves and even animals. In the Ten Commandments the first four are duties to God, the last six are duties to men set out with religious authority.

The Old Testament teaching of 'an eye for an eye' was afterwards criticized as insufficient, and in later times has been regarded as barbaric, though many modern states do little better. For it established the principle of equality before the law, and helped to prevent blood feuds. For injury, only an equal injury should be exacted, the punishment should fit the crime; only one person should be executed for one murder. There was respect for human life, and mutilation was not practised as in some other countries where a hand might be cut off for stealing or an eye plucked out for adultery.

The rights of widows and foreigners were not only maintained in prophecies but written into legislation: 'a stranger shalt thou not wrong . . . for you were strangers'. Slaves were protected from wrongful injury and emancipated after seven years: 'in the seventh year he shall go free for nothing'. In the reform set out under prophetic influence in the book of Deuteronomy, and enacted by king Josiah in 620 B.C., further humane laws were given. Rails should be put round dangerous house-tops, and an enemy's trees were to be spared after conquest. Dumb animals were to be helped; the lost sheep must be returned, the sitting bird must not be disturbed, and the ox should not be muzzled when treading out the corn. So finally Leviticus propounds the Old Testament ideal for social relationships: 'Thou shalt not hate thy brother in thy heart. . . . Thou shalt not take vengeance. . . . Thou shalt love thy neighbour as thyself.'[22]

The New Testament completes this moral and religious development, for the Sermon on the Mount is the climax of ethical monotheism. Out of the multitude of Old Testament and Rabbinic laws two emerge as including all the rest, said Jesus. The first is the Shema, 'Hear, O Israel . . . thou shalt love the Lord thy God with all thy heart, and with all thy soul, and with all thy mind, and with all thy strength.' But the second is like it, love to man like love to God, being of the same nature, 'Thou shalt love thy neighbour as thyself.'[23]

The Sermon on the Mount goes beyond the outward action to the inner motive. Not only killing, but being angry is condemned; not only adultery, but the lustful desire; not swearing but speaking plain truth is taught. The equal retribution of eye for eye is surpassed by turning the other cheek. The old law taught forgiveness, but the new Gospel teaches, 'Love your enemies, do good to them that hate you, bless them that curse you, and pray for them that despitefully use you.'[24]

This is taken up by Paul when he says that all the law 'is summed up in this word, namely, Thou shalt love thy neighbour as thyself'. And James calls this 'the royal law'. But we must beware of thinking of Jesus as a new legislator, a second Moses teaching a higher and even harder law. The new teaching must not be fixed like the old, and must spring from love rather than a sense of duty.[25]

Both the teaching and the life of Jesus show a new way of dealing with evil and overcoming it. Violence is not simply to be met with passive harmlessness, but with active love. 'Resist not the evil one . . . turn the other cheek . . . give your cloak as well . . . go the extra mile . . . lend to the borrower.' Hatred is not to be met with hatred, but with love, prayer and blessing. And all this is because God does it already, he sends rain on the just and the unjust, and is kind to the unthankful and the evil. So, 'be ye merciful, even as your Father is merciful'.[26]

In example as well as precept Jesus showed a new way of human relationships. In his many dealings with social outcasts he was in scorn called 'a friend of publicans and sinners', though it is his glory now. In the agonies of death he prayed for his persecutors and pleaded their ignorance, 'Father, forgive them, for they know not what they do.'[27]

This brought about a new attitude towards the untouchable and traditional enemies. The Samaritan, formerly hated by the Jews, becomes for ever after the Good Samaritan from the teaching of Jesus. Moved with compassion Jesus touched the unclean leper, raised the widow's son, and forgave the harlot; 'her sins, which are many, are forgiven; for she loved much'. It was after eating with tax-gatherers that Jesus quoted the words of Hosea, 'I desire mercy and not sacrifice.' So it was said about him, 'Himself took our infirmities and bore our diseases.' And on the Cross it was rightly said of this most self-forgetting of men, 'He saved others, himself he cannot save.'[28]

The effect of this upon the followers of Jesus was very great. 'Christ left you an example . . . when he was reviled, he reviled not again, when he suffered threatened not', said Peter. And Stephen at his martyrdom prayed like his Master, 'Lord, lay not this sin to their charge'. This teaching was continued by Paul in his exhortations to the Romans, 'Bless them that persecute you, bless and curse not. . . . Render to no man evil for evil. . . . Be at peace with all men. . . . If thine enemy hunger feed him, if he thirst give him to drink. . . . Be not overcome by evil, but overcome evil with good.'[29]

So the Golden Rule of Christianity is given in the Gospels in two forms: 'As you would that men should do to you, do ye to them likewise'; and, 'All things whatsoever you would that men should do unto you, even so do ye also unto them.'[30]

With such strong moral teachings, inextricably mingled with its religion and growing out of it, Christianity must always have a social conscience and sacrifice itself in the service of the poor and distressed. As somebody has said, Christianity has successfully defied the law of the survival of the fittest for twenty centuries, by saving the sick and the poor. Even its enemies have recognized this. Julian the Apostate admitted that Christians cared not only for their own poor but for pagans as well; and Gibbon attributed the triumph of Christianity largely to its high moral standards.

With all the failings of many of its advocates, this concern for social service has remained characteristic of the religion of Christ, and has stimulated other religions to copy it. 'By their fruits ye shall know them' remains the judgement that it passes upon its own life. The claim sometimes made that the West has developed the head but not the heart is disproved by the abundant social works in many countries that come from the religion of Christ. Christianity has been at its best when it has been close to the teaching and example of its Founder, as set out in its sacred scriptures.

Today both Hinduism and Christianity are in close contact and cannot ignore each other's teachings. This contact can be made fruitful if they are willing to learn from each other, for neither has a complete monopoly of the truth. It is important to learn what each teaches, and the foregoing pages have tried to expound some of the principal teachings of Hindu and Christian scriptures. When we understand each other's holy texts, we may have the grace to appreciate each other's strivings after truth and goodness.

References

1. *Religion and Philosophy of the Veda*, p. 584.
2. *Hindu Mysticism*, p. 98 f.
3. Taittirīya Upanishad 1, 11.
4. Chāndogya 8, 8; Kaṭha 1, 23 ff.
5. Bṛihad-āraṇyaka 2, 4; *The Thirteen Principal Upanishads*, p. 65.
6. Bhagavad Gītā 1, 28 ff.
7. *The Bhagavadgītā*, p. 94.
8. Gītā 2, 31.
9. ib. 2, 19.
10. ib. 14, 23 f.; 18, 49 ff.; 14, 25.
11. ib. 12, 13; Radhakrishnan, op. cit., p. 323.
12. *Hindu Mysticism*, p. 99.
13. Laws of Manu 3, 92; 6, 47; Mahābhārata 38, 73, 74.
14. Manu 10, 63.
15. ib. 1, 87; 1, 98; 2, 31.
16. ib. 5, 46; 10, 83 f.
17. Gītā 17, 14; 16, 2 f.
18. *The Path of Light*, tr. L. D. Barnett (Murray, second edition, 1947), pp. 44 f.
19. See Swami Agehananda, *The Ochre Robe* (Allen & Unwin, 1961), pp. 119 ff.
20. Amos 2, 6; 5, 21 f.
21. Hosea 6, 6; Isaiah 1, 15; Micah 6, 8.
22. Deuteronomy 22, 8; 20, 19; 22, 1; 22, 7; 25, 4; Lev. 19, 18.
23. Mark 12, 29 f.
24. Luke 6, 27 f.
25. Romans 13, 9; James 2, 8.
26. Matt. 5, 39 ff.; Luke 6, 36.
27. Luke 7, 34; 23, 34.
28. Luke 7, 47; Matt. 9, 13; 8, 17; 27, 42.
29. 1 Peter 2, 21; Acts 7, 60; Romans 12, 14 f.
30. Luke 6, 31; Matt. 7, 12.

INDEX

INDEX

72 73 74 12 11 10 9 8 7 6 5 4 3 2 1

Revised January, 1970

harper torchbooks

American Studies: General

IENRY ADAMS Degradation of the Democratic Dogma. ‡ *Introduction by Charles Hirschfeld.* TB/1450

OUIS D. BRANDEIS: Other People's Money, *and How the Bankers Use It. Ed. with Intro, by Richard M. Abrams* TB/3081

IENRY STEELE COMMAGER, Ed.: The Struggle for Racial Equality TB/1300

ARL N. DEGLER: Out of Our Past: *The Forces that Shaped Modern America* CN/2

ARL N. DEGLER, Ed.: Pivotal Interpretations of American History
Vol. I TB/1240; Vol. II TB/1241

. S. EISENSTADT, Ed.: The Craft of American History: *Selected Essays*
Vol. I TB/1255; Vol. II TB/1256

AWRENCE H. FUCHS, Ed.: American Ethnic Politics TB/1368

IARCUS LEE HANSEN: The Atlantic Migration: 1607-1860. *Edited by Arthur M. Schlesinger. Introduction by Oscar Handlin* TB/1052

IARCUS LEE HANSEN: The Immigrant in American History. *Edited with a Foreword by Arthur M. Schlesinger* TB/1120

OBERT L. HEILBRONER: The Limits of American Capitalism TB/1305

OHN HIGHAM, Ed.: The Reconstruction of American History TB/1068

OBERT H. JACKSON: The Supreme Court in the American System of Government TB/1106

OHN F. KENNEDY: A Nation of Immigrants. *Illus. Revised and Enlarged. Introduction by Robert F. Kennedy* TB/1118

EONARD W. LEVY, Ed.: American Constitutional Law: *Historical Essays* TB/1285

EONARD W. LEVY, Ed.: Judicial Review and the Supreme Court TB/1296

EONARD W. LEVY: The Law of the Commonwealth and Chief Justice Shaw: *The Evolution of American Law, 1830-1860* TB/1309

ORDON K. LEWIS: Puerto Rico: *Freedom and Power in the Caribbean. Abridged edition* TB/1371

UNNAR MYRDAL: An American Dilemma: *The Negro Problem and Modern Democracy. Introduction by the Author.*
Vol. I TB/1443; Vol. II TB/1444

LBERT OSOFSKY, Ed.: The Burden of Race: *A Documentary History of Negro-White Relations in America* TB/1405

ARNOLD ROSE: The Negro in America: *The Condensed Version of Gunnar Myrdal's* An American Dilemma. *Second Edition* TB/3048

JOHN E. SMITH: Themes in American Philosophy: *Purpose, Experience and Community* TB/1466

WILLIAM R. TAYLOR: Cavalier and Yankee: *The Old South and American National Character* TB/1474

American Studies: Colonial

BERNARD BAILYN: The New England Merchants in the Seventeenth Century TB/1149

ROBERT E. BROWN: Middle-Class Democracy and Revolution in Massachusetts, 1691–1780. *New Introduction by Author* TB/1413

JOSEPH CHARLES: The Origins of the American Party System TB/1049

WESLEY FRANK CRAVEN: The Colonies in Transition: 1660-1712† TB/3084

CHARLES GIBSON: Spain in America † TB/3077

CHARLES GIBSON, Ed.: The Spanish Tradition in America + HR/1351

LAWRENCE HENRY GIPSON: The Coming of the Revolution: 1763-1775. † *Illus.* TB/3007

JACK P. GREENE, Ed.: Great Britain and the American Colonies: 1606-1763. + *Introduction by the Author* HR/1477

AUBREY C. LAND, Ed.: Bases of the Plantation Society + HR/1429

PERRY MILLER: Errand Into the Wilderness TB/1139

PERRY MILLER & T. H. JOHNSON, Ed.: The Puritans: *A Sourcebook of Their Writings*
Vol. I TB/1093; Vol. II TB/1094

EDMUND S. MORGAN: The Puritan Family: *Religion and Domestic Relations in Seventeenth Century New England* TB/1227

WALLACE NOTESTEIN: The English People on the Eve of Colonization: 1603-1630. † *Illus.* TB/3006

LOUIS B. WRIGHT: The Cultural Life of the American Colonies: 1607-1763. † *Illus.* TB/3005

YVES F. ZOLTVANY, Ed.: The French Tradition in America + HR/1425

American Studies: The Revolution to 1860

JOHN R. ALDEN: The American Revolution: 1775-1783. † *Illus.* TB/3011

The New American Nation Series, edited by Henry Steele Commager and Richard B. Morris.
American Perspectives series, edited by Bernard Wishy and William E. Leuchtenburg.
History of Europe series, edited by J. H. Plumb.
The Library of Religion and Culture, edited by Benjamin Nelson.
Researches in the Social, Cultural, and Behavioral Sciences, edited by Benjamin Nelson.
Harper Modern Science Series, edited by James A. Newman.
Not for sale in Canada.
· Documentary History of the United States series, edited by Richard B. Morris.
Documentary History of Western Civilization series, edited by Eugene C. Black and Leonard W. Levy.
The Economic History of the United States series, edited by Henry David et al.
European Perspectives series, edited by Eugene C. Black.
* Contemporary Essays series, edited by Leonard W. Levy.
The Stratum Series, edited by John Hale.

RAY A. BILLINGTON: The Far Western Frontier: 1830-1860. † *Illus.* TB/3012

STUART BRUCHEY: The Roots of American Economic Growth, 1607-1861: *An Essay in Social Causation. New Introduction by the Author.* TB/1350

WHITNEY R. CROSS: The Burned-Over District: *The Social and Intellectual History of Enthusiastic Religion in Western New York, 1800-1850* TB/1242

NOBLE E. CUNNINGHAM, JR., Ed.: The Early Republic, 1789-1828 + HR/1394

GEORGE DANGERFIELD: The Awakening of American Nationalism, 1815-1828. † *Illus.* TB/3061

CLEMENT EATON: The Freedom-of-Thought Struggle in the Old South. *Revised and Enlarged. Illus.* TB/1150

CLEMENT EATON: The Growth of Southern Civilization, 1790-1860. † *Illus.* TB/3040

ROBERT H. FERRELL, Ed.: Foundations of American Diplomacy, 1775-1872 + HR/1393

LOUIS FILLER: The Crusade against Slavery: 1830-1860. † *Illus.* TB/3029

DAVID H. FISCHER: The Revolution of American Conservatism: *The Federalist Party in the Era of Jeffersonian Democracy* TB/1449

WILLIM W. FREEHLING: Prelude to Civil War: *The Nullification Controversy in South Carolina, 1816-1836* TB/1359

PAUL W. GATES: The Farmer's Age: *Agriculture, 1815-1860* Δ TB/1398

THOMAS JEFFERSON: Notes on the State of Virginia. ‡ *Edited by Thomas P. Abernethy* TB/3052

FORREST MCDONALD, Ed.: Confederation and Constitution, 1781-1789 + HR/1396

BERNARD MAYO: Myths and Men: *Patrick Henry, George Washington, Thomas Jefferson* TB/1108

JOHN C. MILLER: Alexander Hamilton and the Growth of the New Nation TB/3057

JOHN C. MILLER: The Federalist Era: 1789-1801. † *Illus.* TB/3027

RICHARD B. MORRIS, Ed.: Alexander Hamilton and the Founding of the Nation. *New Introduction by the Editor* TB/1448

RICHARD B. MORRIS: The American Revolution Reconsidered TB/1363

CURTIS P. NETTELS: The Emergence of a National Economy, 1775-1815 Δ TB/1438

DOUGLASS C. NORTH & ROBERT PAUL THOMAS, Eds.: *The Growth of the American Economy to 1860* + HR/1352

R. B. NYE: The Cultural Life of the New Nation: 1776-1830. † *Illus.* TB/3026

GILBERT OSOFSKY, Ed.: Puttin' On Ole Massa: *The Slave Narratives of Henry Bibb, William Wells Brown, and Solomon Northup* ‡ TB/1432

JAMES PARTON: The Presidency of Andrew Jackson. *From Volume III of the* Life of Andrew Jackson. *Ed. with Intro. by Robert V. Remini* TB/3080

FRANCIS S. PHILBRICK: The Rise of the West, 1754-1830. † *Illus.* TB/3067

MARSHALL SMELSER: The Democratic Republic, 1801-1815 † TB/1406

JACK M. SOSIN, Ed.: The Opening of the West + HR/1424

GEORGE ROGERS TAYLOR: The Transportation Revolution, 1815-1860 Δ TB/1347

A. F. TYLER: Freedom's Ferment: *Phases of American Social History from the Revolution to the Outbreak of the Civil War. Illus.* TB/1074

GLYNDON G. VAN DEUSEN: The Jacksonian Era: 1828-1848. † *Illus.* TB/3028

LOUIS B. WRIGHT: Culture on the Moving Frontier TB/1053

American Studies: The Civil War to 1900

W. R. BROCK: An American Crisis: *Congress and Reconstruction, 1865-67* ° TB/1283

T. C. COCHRAN & WILLIAM MILLER: The Age of Enterprise: *A Social History of Industrial America* TB/1054

W. A. DUNNING: Reconstruction, Political and Economic: 1865-1877 TB/1073

HAROLD U. FAULKNER: Politics, Reform and Expansion: 1890-1900. † *Illus.* TB/3020

GEORGE M. FREDRICKSON: The Inner Civil War: *Northern Intellectuals and the Crisis of the Union* TB/1358

JOHN A. GARRATY: The New Commonwealth, 1877-1890 † TB/1410

JOHN A. GARRATY, Ed.: The Transformation of American Society, 1870-1890 + HR/1395

HELEN HUNT JACKSON: A Century of Dishonor: *The Early Crusade for Indian Reform.* † *Edited by Andrew F. Rolle* TB/3063

WILLIAM G. MCLOUGHLIN, Ed.: The American Evangelicals, 1800-1900: An Anthology ‡ TB/1382

ARNOLD M. PAUL: Conservative Crisis and the Rule of Law: *Attitudes of Bar and Bench, 1887-1895. New Introduction by Author* TB/1415

JAMES S. PIKE: The Prostrate State: *South Carolina under Negro Government.* ‡ *Intro. by Robert F. Durden* TB/3085

WHITELAW REID: After the War: *A Tour of the Southern States, 1865-1866.* ‡ *Edited by C. Vann Woodward* TB/3066

FRED A. SHANNON: The Farmer's Last Frontier: *Agriculture, 1860-1897* TB/1348

VERNON LANE WHARTON: The Negro in Mississippi, 1865-1890 TB/1178

American Studies: The Twentieth Century

RICHARD M. ABRAMS, Ed.: The Issues of the Populist and Progressive Eras, 1892-1912 + HR/1428

RAY STANNARD BAKER: Following the Color Line: *American Negro Citizenship in Progressive Era.* ‡ *Edited by Dewey W. Grantham, Jr. Illus.* TB/3053

RANDOLPH S. BOURNE: War and the Intellectuals: *Collected Essays, 1915-1919.* ‡ *Edited by Carl Resek* TB/3043

A. RUSSELL BUCHANAN: The United States and World War II. † *Illus.* Vol. I TB/3044; Vol. II TB/3045

THOMAS C. COCHRAN: The American Business System: *A Historical Perspective, 1900-1955* TB/1080

FOSTER RHEA DULLES: America's Rise to World Power: 1898-1954. † *Illus.* TB/3021

JEAN-BAPTISTE DUROSELLE: From Wilson to Roosevelt: *Foreign Policy of the United States, 1913-1945. Trans. by Nancy Lyman Roelker* TB/1370

HAROLD U. FAULKNER: The Decline of Laissez Faire, 1897-1917 TB/1397

JOHN D. HICKS: Republican Ascendancy: 1921-1933. † *Illus.* TB/3041

WILLIAM E. LEUCHTENBURG: Franklin D. Roosevelt and the New Deal: 1932-1940. † *Illus.* TB/3025

WILLIAM E. LEUCHTENBURG, Ed.: The New Deal: *A Documentary History* + HR/1354

ARTHUR S. LINK: Woodrow Wilson and the Progressive Era: 1910-1917. † *Illus.* TB/3023

BROADUS MITCHELL: Depression Decade: *From New Era through New Deal, 1929-1941* ^ TB/1439

GEORGE E. MOWRY: The Era of Theodore Roosevelt and the Birth of Modern America: 1900-1912. † *Illus.* TB/3022

WILLIAM PRESTON, JR.: Aliens and Dissenters: *Federal Suppression of Radicals, 1903-1933* TB/1287

WALTER RAUSCHENBUSCH: Christianity and the Social Crisis. ‡ *Edited by Robert D. Cross* TB/3059

GEORGE SOULE: Prosperity Decade: *From War to Depression, 1917-1929* Δ TB/1349

GEORGE B. TINDALL, Ed.: A Populist Reader: *Selections from the Works of American Populist Leaders* TB/3069

TWELVE SOUTHERNERS: I'll Take My Stand: *The South and the Agrarian Tradition. Intro. by Louis D. Rubin, Jr.; Biographical Essays by Virginia Rock* TB/1072

Art, Art History, Aesthetics

CREIGHTON GILBERT, Ed.: Renaissance Art ** *Illus.* TB/1465

EMILE MALE: The Gothic Image: *Religious Art in France of the Thirteenth Century. § 190* illus. TB/344

MILLARD MEISS: Painting in Florence and Siena After the Black Death: *The Arts, Religion and Society in the Mid-Fourteenth Century. 169 illus.* TB/1148

ERWIN PANOFSKY: Renaissance and Renascences in Western Art. *Illus.* TB/1447

ERWIN PANOFSKY: Studies in Iconology: *Humanistic Themes in the Art of the Renaissance. 180 illus.* TB/1077

OTTO VON SIMSON: The Gothic Cathedral: *Origins of Gothic Architecture and the Medieval Concept of Order. 58 illus.* TB/2018

HEINRICH ZIMMER: Myths and Symbols in Indian Art and Civilization. *70 illus.* TB/2005

Asian Studies

WOLFGANG FRANKE: China and the West: *The Cultural Encounter, 13th to 20th Centuries. Trans. by R. A. Wilson* TB/1326

L. CARRINGTON GOODRICH: A Short History of the Chinese People. *Illus.* TB/3015

DAN N. JACOBS, Ed.: The New Communist Manifesto and Related Documents. TB/1078

DAN N. JACOBS & HANS H. BAERWALD, Eds.: Chinese Communism: *Selected Documents* TB/3031

BENJAMIN I. SCHWARTZ: Chinese Communism and the Rise of Mao TB/1308

BENJAMIN I. SCHWARTZ: In Search of Wealth and Power: *Yen Fu and the West* TB/1422

Economics & Economic History

C. E. BLACK: The Dynamics of Modernization: *A Study in Comparative History* TB/1321

STUART BRUCHEY: The Roots of American Economic Growth, 1607-1861: *An Essay in Social Causation. New Introduction by the Author.* TB/1350

GILBERT BURCK & EDITORS OF *Fortune:* The Computer Age: *And its Potential for Management* TB/1179

SHEPARD B. CLOUGH, THOMAS MOODIE & CAROL MOODIE, Eds.: Economic History of Europe: *Twentieth Century #* HR/1388

THOMAS C. COCHRAN: The American Business System: *A Historical Perspective, 1900-1955* TB/1080

ROBERT A. DAHL & CHARLES E. LINDBLOM: Politics, Economics, and Welfare: *Planning and Politico-Economic Systems Resolved into Basic Social Processes* TB/3037

PETER F. DRUCKER: The New Society: *The Anatomy of Industrial Order* TB/1082

HAROLD U. FAULKNER: The Decline of Laissez Faire, 1897-1917 Δ TB/1397

PAUL W. GATES: The Farmer's Age: *Agriculture, 1815-1860* Δ TB/1398

WILLIAM GREENLEAF, Ed.: American Economic Development Since 1860 + HR/1353

ROBERT L. HEILBRONER: The Future as History: *The Historic Currents of Our Time and the Direction in Which They Are Taking America* TB/1386

ROBERT L. HEILBRONER: The Great Ascent: *The Struggle for Economic Development in Our Time* TB/3030

DAVID S. LANDES: Bankers and Pashas: *International Finance and Economic Imperialism in Egypt. New Preface by the Author* TB/1412

ROBERT LATOUCHE: The Birth of Western Economy: *Economic Aspects of the Dark Ages* TB/1290

W. ARTHUR LEWIS: The Principles of Economic Planning. *New Introduction by the Author°* TB/1436

WILLIAM MILLER, Ed.: Men in Business: *Essays on the Historical Role of the Entrepreneur* TB/1081

GUNNAR MYRDAL: An International Economy. *New Introduction by the Author* TB/1445

HERBERT A. SIMON: The Shape of Automation: *For Men and Management* TB/1245

RICHARD S. WECKSTEIN, Ed.: Expansion of World Trade and the Growth of National Economies ** TB/1373

Historiography and History of Ideas

J. BRONOWSKI & BRUCE MAZLISH: The Western Intellectual Tradition: *From Leonardo to Hegel* TB/3001

WILHELM DILTHEY: Pattern and Meaning in History: *Thoughts on History and Society.° Edited with an Intro. by H. P. Rickman* TB/1075

J. H. HEXTER: More's Utopia: *The Biography of an Idea. Epilogue by the Author* TB/1195

H. STUART HUGHES: History as Art and as Science: *Twin Vistas on the Past* TB/1207

ARTHUR O. LOVEJOY: The Great Chain of Being: *A Study of the History of an Idea* TB/1009

RICHARD H. POPKIN: The History of Scepticism from Erasmus to Descartes. *Revised Edition* TB/1391

MASSIMO SALVADORI, Ed.: Modern Socialism # HR/1374

BRUNO SNELL: The Discovery of the Mind: *The Greek Origins of European Thought* TB/1018

W. WARREN WAGER, ed.: European Intellectual History Since Darwin and Marx TB/1297

History: General

HANS KOHN: The Age of Nationalism: *The First Era of Global History* TB/1380

BERNARD LEWIS: The Arabs in History TB/1029

BERNARD LEWIS: The Middle East and the West ° TB/1274

History: Ancient

A. ANDREWS: The Greek Tyrants TB/1103

ERNST LUDWIG EHRLICH: A Concise History of Israel: *From the Earliest Times to the Destruction of the Temple in A.D. 70* ° TB/128
THEODOR H. GASTER: Thespis: *Ritual Myth and Drama in the Ancient Near East* TB/1281
MICHAEL GRANT: Ancient History ° TB/1190
A. H. M. JONES, Ed.: A History of Rome through the Fifth Century # *Vol. I: The Republic* HR/1364
Vol. II The Empire: HR/1460
NAPHTALI LEWIS & MEYER REINHOLD, Eds.: Roman Civilization *Vol. I: The Republic* TB/1231
Vol. II: The Empire TB/1232

History: Medieval

MARSHALL W. BALDWIN, Ed.: Christianity Through the 13th Century # HR/1468
MARC BLOCH: Land and Work in Medieval Europe. *Translated by J. E. Anderson* TB/1452
HELEN CAM: England Before Elizabeth TB/1026
NORMAN COHN: The Pursuit of the Millennium: *Revolutionary Messianism in Medieval and Reformation Europe* TB/1037
G. G. COULTON: Medieval Village, Manor, and Monastery HR/1022
HEINRICH FICHTENAU: The Carolingian Empire: *The Age of Charlemagne. Translated with an Introduction by Peter Munz* TB/1142
GALBERT OF BRUGES: The Murder of Charles the Good: *A Contemporary Record of Revolutionary Change in 12th Century Flanders. Translated with an Introduction by James Bruce Ross* TB/1311
F. L. GANSHOF: Feudalism TB/1058
F. L. GANSHOF: The Middle Ages: *A History of International Relations. Translated by Rêmy Hall* TB/1411
DENYS HAY: The Medieval Centuries ° TB/1192
DAVID HERLIHY, Ed.: Medieval Culture and Socitey # HR/1340
J. M. HUSSEY: The Byzantine World TB/1057
ROBERT LATOUCHE: The Birth of Western Economy: *Economic Aspects of the Dark Ages* ° TB/1290
HENRY CHARLES LEA: The Inquisition of the Middle Ages. || *Introduction by Walter Ullmann* TB/1456
FERDINARD LOT: The End of the Ancient World and the Beginnings of the Middle Ages. *Introduction by Glanville Downey* TB/1044
H. R. LOYN: The Norman Conquest TB/1457
ACHILLE LUCHAIRE: Social France at the time of Philip Augustus. *Intro. by John W. Baldwin* TB/1314
GUIBERT DE NOGENT: Self and Society in Medieval France: *The Memoirs of Guibert de Nogent.* || Edited by John F. Benton TB/1471
MARSILIUS OF PADUA: The Defender of Peace. *The* Defensor Pacis. *Translated with an Introduction by Alan Gewirth* TB/1310
CHARLES PETET-DUTAILLIS: The Feudal Monarchy in France and England: *From the Tenth to the Thirteenth Century* ° TB/1165
STEVEN RUNCIMAN: A History of the Crusades Vol. I: *The First Crusade and the Foundation of the Kingdom of Jerusalem. Illus.* TB/1143
Vol. II: *The Kingdom of Jerusalem and the Frankish East 1100-1187. Illus.* TB/1243
Vol. III: *The Kingdom of Acre and the Later Crusades. Illus.* TB/1298
J. M. WALLACE-HADRILL: The Barbarian West: *The Early Middle Ages, A.D. 400-1000* TB/1061

History: Renaissance & Reformation

JACOB BURCKHARDT: The Civilization of the Renaissance in Italy. *Introduction by Benjamin Nelson and Charles Trinkaus. Illus.* Vol. I TB/40; Vol. II TB/41
JOHN CALVIN & JACOPO SADOLETO: A Reformation Debate. *Edited by John C. Olin* TB/1239
FEDERICO CHABOD: Machiavelli and the Renaissance TB/1193
J. H. ELLIOTT: Europe Divided, 1559-1598 *a* ° TB/1414
G. R. ELTON: Reformation Europe, 1517-1559 ° *a* TB/1270
DESIDERIUS ERASMUS: Christian Humanism and the Reformation: *Selected Writings. Edited and Translated by John C. Olin* TB/1166
DESIDERIUS ERASMUS: Erasmus and His Age: *Selected Letters. Edited with an Introduction by Hans J. Hillerbrand. Translated by Marcus A. Haworth* TB/1461
WALLACE K. FERGUSON et al.: Facets of the Renaissance TB/1098
WALLACE K. FERGUSON et al.: The Renaissance: *Six Essays. Illus.* TB/1084
FRANCESCO GUICCIARDINI: History of Florence. *Translated with an Introduction and Notes by Mario Domandi* TB/1470
WERNER L. GUNDERSHEIMER, Ed.: French Humanism, 1470-1600. * *Illus.* TB/1473
MARIE BOAS HALL, Ed.: Nature and Nature's Laws: *Documents of the Scientific Revolution #* HR/1420
HANS J. HILLERBRAND, Ed., The Protestant Reformation # TB/1342
JOHAN HUIZINGA: Erasmus and the Age of Reformation. *Illus.* TB/19
JOEL HURSTFIELD: The Elizabethan Nation TB/1312
JOEL HURSTFIELD, Ed.: The Reformation Crisis TB/1267
PAUL OSKAR KRISTELLER: Renaissance Thought: *The Classic, Scholastic, and Humanist Strains* TB/1048
PAUL OSKAR KRISTELLER: Renaissance Thought II: *Papers on Humanism and the Arts* TB/1163
PAUL O. KRISTELLER & PHILIP P. WIENER, Eds.: Renaissance Essays TB/1392
DAVID LITTLE: Religion, Order and Law: *A Study in Pre-Revolutionary England. § Preface by R. Bellah* TB/1418
NICCOLO MACHIAVELLI: History of Florence and of the Affairs of Italy: *From the Earliest Times to the Death of Lorenzo the Magnificent. Introduction by Felix Gilbert* TB/1027
ALFRED VON MARTIN: Sociology of the Renaissance. ° *Introduction by W. K. Ferguson* TB/1099
GARRETT MATTINGLY et al.: Renaissance Profiles. *Edited by J. H. Plumb* TB/1162
J. H. PARRY: The Establishment of the European Hegemony: 1415-1715: *Trade and Exploration in the Age of the Renaissance* TB/1045
J. H. PARRY, Ed.: The European Reconnaissance: *Selected Documents #* HR/1345
J. H. PLUMB: The Italian Renaissance: *A Concise Survey of Its History and Culture* TB/1161
A. F. POLLARD: Henry VIII. *Introductioh by A. G. Dickens.* ° TB/1249
RICHARD H. POPKIN: The History of Scepticism from Erasmus to Descartes TB/1391
PAOLO ROSSI: Philosophy, Technology, and the Arts, in the Early Modern Era 1400-1700. || *Edited by Benjamin Nelson. Translated by Salvator Attanasio* TB/1458

R. H. TAWNEY: The Agrarian Problem in the Sixteenth Century. *Intro. by Lawrence Stone* TB/1315

H. R. TREVOR-ROPER: The European Witch-craze of the Sixteenth and Seventeenth Centuries and Other Essays ° TB/1416

VESPASIANO: Rennaissance Princes, Popes, and *XVth Century: The Vespasiano Memoirs. Introduction by Myron P. Gilmore. Illus.* TB/1111

History: Modern European

RENE ALBRECHT-CARRIE, Ed.: The Concert of Europe # HR/1341

MAX BELOFF: The Age of Absolutism, 1660-1815 TB/1062

OTTO VON BISMARCK: Reflections and Reminiscences. *Ed. with Intro. by Theodore S. Hamerow* ¶ TB/1357

EUGENE C. BLACK, Ed.: British Politics in the Nineteenth Century # HR/1427

D. W. BROGAN: The Development of Modern France ° Vol. I: *From the Fall of the Empire to the Dreyfus Affair* TB/1184 Vol. II: *The Shadow of War, World War I, Between the Two Wars* TB/1185

ALAN BULLOCK: Hitler, A Study in Tyranny. ° *Revised Edition. Iuus.* TB/1123

GORDON A. CRAIG: From Bismarck to Adenauer: *Aspects of German Statecraft. Revised Edition* TB/1171

LESTER G. CROCKER, Ed.: The Age of Enlightenment # HR/1423

JACQUES DROZ: Europe between Revolutions, 1815-1848. ° *a Trans. by Robert Baldick* TB/1346

JOHANN GOTTLIEB FICHTE: Addresses to the German Nation. *Ed. with Intro. by George A. Kelly* ¶ TB/1366

ROBERT & ELBORG FORSTER, Eds.: European Society in the Eighteenth Century # HR/1404

C. C. GILLISPIE: Genesis and Geology: *The Decades before Darwin* § TB/51

ALBERT GOODWIN: The French Revolution TB/1064

JOHN B. HALSTED, Ed.: Romanticism # HR/1387

STANLEY HOFFMANN et al.: In Search of France: *The Economy, Society and Political System In the Twentieth Century* TB/1219

H. STUART HUGHES: The Obstructed Path: *French Social Thought in the Years of Desperation* TB/1451

JOHAN HUIZINGA: Dutch Civilisation in the 17th Century and Other Essays TB/1453

WALTER LAQUEUR & GEORGE L. MOSSE, Eds.: Education and Social Structure in the 20th Century. ° *Volume 6 of the* Journal of Contemporary History TB/1339

WALTER LAQUEUR & GEORGE L. MOSSE, Ed.: International Fascism, 1920-1945. ° *Volume 1 of the* Journal of Contemporary History TB/1276

WALTER LAQUEUR & GEORGE L. MOSSE, Eds.: Literature and Politics in the 20th Century. ° *Volume 5 of the* Journal of Contemporary History. TB/1328

WALTER LAQUEUR & GEORGE L. MOSSE, Eds.: The New History: *Trends in Historical Research and Writing Since World War II.* ° *Volume 4 of the* Journal of Contemporary History TB/1327

WALTER LAQUEUR & GEORGE L. MOSSE, Eds.: 1914: *The Coming of the First World War.* ° *Volume3 of the* Journal of Contemporary *History* TB/1306

JOHN MCMANNERS: European History, 1789-1914: *Men, Machines and Freedom* TB/1419

PAUL MANTOUX: The Industrial Revolution in the Eighteenth Century: *An Outline of the Beginnings of the Modern Factory System in England* TB/1079

KINGSLEY MARTIN: French Liberal Thought in the Eighteenth Century: *A Study of Political Ideas from Bayle to Condorcet* TB/1114

NAPOLEON III: Napoleonic Ideas: *Des Idées Napoléoniennes, par le Prince Napoléon-Louis Bonaparte. Ed. by Brison D. Gooch* ¶ TB/1336

FRANZ NEUMANN: Behemoth: *The Structure and Practice of National Socialism, 1933-1944* TB/1289

DAVID OGG: Europe of the Ancien Régime, 1715-1783 ° *a* TB/1271

GEORGE RUDE: Revolutionary Europe, 1783-1815 ° *a* TB/1272

MASSIMO SALVADORI, Ed.: Modern Socialism # TB/1374

DENIS MACK SMITH, Ed.: The Making of Italy, 1796-1870 # HR/1356

ALBERT SOREL: Europe Under the Old Regime, *Translated by Francis H. Herrick* TB/1121

ROLAND N. STROMBERG, Ed.: Realsim, Naturalism, and Symbolism: *Modes of Thought and Expression in Europe, 1848-1914 #* HR/1355

A. J. P. TAYLOR: From Napoleon to Lenin: *Historical Essays* ° TB/1268

A. J. P. TAYLOR: The Habsburg Monarchy, 1809-1918: *A History of the Austrian Empire and Austria-Hungary* ° TB/1187

J. M. THOMPSON: European History, 1494-1789 TB/1431

DAVID THOMSON, Ed.: France: Empire and Republic, 1850-1940 # HR/1387

H. R. TREVOR-ROPER: Historical Essays TB/1269

W. WARREN WAGAR, Ed.: Science, Faith, and MAN: *European Thought Since 1914 #* HR/1362

MACK WALKER, Ed.: Metternich's Europe, 1813-1848 # HR/1361

ELIZABETH WISKEMANN: Europe of the Dictators, 1919-1945 ° *a* TB/1273

JOHN B. WOLF: France: 1814-1919: *The Rise of a Liberal-Democratic Society* TB/3019

Literature & Literary Criticism

JACQUES BARZUN: The House of Intellect TB/1051

W. J. BATE: From Classic to Romantic: *Premises of Taste in Eighteenth Century England* TB/1036

VAN WYCK BROOKS: Van Wyck Brooks: The Early Years: *A Selection from his Works, 1908-1921 Ed. with Intro. by Claire Sprague* TB/3082

RICHMOND LATTIMORE, Translator: The Odyssey of Homer TB/1389

ROBERT PREYER, Ed.: Victorian Literature ** TB/1302

BASIL WILEY: Nineteenth Century Studies: *Coleridge to Matthew Arnold* ° TB/1261

RAYMOND WILLIAMS: Culture and Society, 1780-1950 ° TB/1252

Philosophy

HENRI BERGSON: Time and Free Will: *An Essay on the Immediate Data of Consciousness* ° TB/1021

LUDWIG BINSWANGER: Being-in-the-World: *Selected Papers. Trans. with Intro. by Jacob Needleman* TB/1365

H. J. BLACKHAM: Six Existentialist Thinkers: *Kierkegaard, Nietzsche, Jaspers, Marcel, Heidegger, Sartre* ° TB/1002

J. M. BOCHENSKI: The Methods of Contemporary Thought. *Trans. by Peter Caws* TB/1377
CRANE BRINTON: Nietzsche. *Preface, Bibliography, and Epilogue by the Author* TB/1197
ERNST CASSIRER: Rousseau, Kant and Goethe. *Intro. by Peter Gay* TB/1092
FREDERICK COPLESTON, *S. J.*: Medieval Philosophy TB/376
F. M. CORNFORD: From Religion to Philosophy: *A Study in the Origins of Western Speculation* § TB/20
WILFRID DESAN: The Tragic Finale: *An Essay on the Philosophy of Jean-Paul Sartre* TB/1030
MARVIN FARBER: The Aims of Phenomenology: *The Motives, Methods, and Impact of Husserl's Thought* TB/1291
PAUL FRIEDLANDER: Plato: *An Introduction* TB/2017
MICHAEL GELVEN: A Commentary on Heidegger's "Being and Time" TB/1464
J. GLENN GRAY: Hegel and Greek Thought TB/1409
W. K. C. GUTHRIE: The Greek Philosophers: *From Thales to Aristotle* ° TB/1008
G. W. F. HEGEL: On Art, Religion Philosophy: *Introductory Lectures to the Realm of Absolute Spirit.* || *Edited with an Introduction by J. Glenn Gray* TB/1463
G. W. F. HEGEL: Phenomenology of Mind. ° || *Introduction by George Lichtheim* TB/1303
MARTIN HEIDEGGER: Discourse on Thinking. *Translated with a Preface by John M. Anderson and E. Hans Freund. Introduction by John M. Anderson* TB/1459
F. H. HEINEMANN: Existentialism and the Modern Predicament TB/28
WERER HEISENBERG: Physics and Philosophy: *The Revolution in Modern Science. Intro. by F. S. C. Nortrop* TB/549
EDMUND HUSSERL: Phenomenology and the Crisis of Philosophy. § *Translated with an Introduction by Quentin Lauer* TB/1170
IMMANUEL KANT: Groundwork of the Metaphysic of Morals. *Translated and Analyzed by H. J. Paton* TB/1159
IMMANUEL KANT: Lectures on Ethics. § *Introduction by Lewis White Beck* TB/105
QUENTIN LAUER: Phenomenology: *Its Genesis and Prospect. Preface by Aron Gurwitsch* TB/1169
GEORGE A. MORGAN: What Nietzsche Means TB/1198
H. J. PATON: The Categorical Imperative: *A Study in Kant's Moral Philosophy* TB/1325
MICHAEL POLANYI: Personal Knowledge: *Towards a Post-Critical Philosophy* TB/1158
KARL R. POPPER: Conjectures and Refutations: *The Growth of Scientific Knowledge* TB/1376
WILLARD VAN ORMAN QUINE: Elementary Logic *Revised Edition* TB/577
MORTON WHITE: Foundations of Historical Knowledge TB/1440
WILHELM WINDELBAND: A History of Philosophy
Vol. I: Greek, Roman, Medieval TB/38
Vol. II: Renaissance, Enlightenment, Modern TB/39
LUDWIG WITTGENSTEIN: The Blue and Brown Books ° TB/1211
LUDWIG WITTGENSTEIN: Notebooks, 1914-1916 TB/1441

Political Science & Government

C. E. BLACK: The Dynamics of Modernization: *A Study in Comparative History* TB/1321
KENNETH E. BOULDING: Conflict and Defense: *A General Theory of Action* TB/3024
DENIS W. BROGAN: Politics in America. *Ne Introduction by the Author* TB/146
ROBERT CONQUEST: Power and Policy in th USSR: *The Study of Soviet Dynastics* ° TB/130
ROBERT A. DAHL & CHARLES E. LINDBLOM: Politics Economics, and Welfare: *Planning and Pc litico-Economic Systems Resolved into Basi Social Processes* TB/127
HANS KOHN: Political Ideologies of the 20t Century TB/127
ROY C. MACRIDIS, Ed.: Political Parties: *Cor temporary Trends and Ideas* ** TB/132
ROBERT GREEN MC CLOSKEY: American Conserva tism in the Age of Enterprise, 1865-1910 TB/113
BARRINGTON MOORE, JR.: Political Power an Social Theory: *Seven Studies* || TB/122
BARRINGTON MOORE, JR.: Soviet Politics—Th Dilemma of Power: *The Role of Ideas i Social Change* || TB/122
BARRINGTON MOORE, JR.: Terror and Progress USSR: *Some Sources of Change and Stabili in the Soviet Dictatorship* TB/126
JOHN B. MORRALL: Political Thought in Mediev Times TB/107
KARL R. POPPER: The Open Society and I Enemies *Vol. I: The Spell of Plato* TB/11C
Vol. II: The High Tide of Prophecy: Hege Marx, and the Aftermath TB/11C
HENRI DE SAINT-SIMON: Social Organization, Th Science of Man, and Other Writings. *Edited and Translated with an Introductic by Felix Markham* TB/115
JOSEPH A. SCHUMPETER: Capitalism, Socialis and Democracy TB/30C

Psychology

LUDWIG BINSWANGER: Being-in-the-world: *S lected papers.* || *Trans. with Intro. by Jacc Needleman* TB/136
HADLEY CANTRIL: The Invasion from Mars: *Study in the Psychology of Panic* || TB/128
MIRCEA ELIADE: Cosmos and History: *The My of the Eternal Return* § TB/205
MIRCEA ELIADE: Myth and Reality TB/136
MIRCEA ELIADE: Myths, Dreams and Mysterie *The Encounter Between Contemporary Fait and Archaic Realities* § TB/132
MIRCEA ELIADE: Rites and Symbols of Initiatior *The Mysteries of Birth and Rebirth* § TB/12
HERBERT FINGARETTE: The Self in Transform tion: *Psychoanalysis, Philosophy and the Li of the Spirit* || TB/11
SIGMUND FREUD: On Creativity and the Unco scious: *Papers on the Psychology of A Literature, Love, Religion.* § *Intro. by Be jamin Nelson* TB/
J. GLENN GRAY: The Warriors: *Reflections Men in Battle. Introduction by Hann Arendt* TB/12
WILLIAM JAMES: Psychology: *The Brief Course. Edited with an Intro. by Gord Allport* TB/10
MUZAFER SHERIF: The Psychology of Soc Norms. *Introduction by Gardner Murphy* TB/30
HELLMUT WILHELM: Change: *Eight Lectures the* I Ching TB/20

Religion: Ancient and Classical, Biblical a Judaic Traditions

C. K. BARRETT, Ed.: The New Testament Bac ground: *Selected Documents* TB/

MARTIN BUBER: Eclipse of God: *Studies in the Relation Between Religion and Philosophy* TB/12
MARTIN BUBER: Hasidism and Modern Man. *Edited and Translated by Maurice Friedman* TB/839
MARTIN BUBER: The Knowledge of Man. *Edited with an Introduction by Maurice Friedman. Translated by Maurice Friedman and Ronald Gregor Smith* TB/135
MARTIN BUBER: Moses. *The Revelation and the Covenant* TB/837
MARTIN BUBER: The Origin and Meaning of Hasidism. *Edited and Translated by Maurice Friedman* TB/835
MARTIN BUBER: The Prophetic Faith TB/73
MARTIN BUBER: Two Types of Faith: *Interpenetration of Judaism and Christianity* ° TB/75
MALCOLM L. DIAMOND: Martin Buber: *Jewish Existentialist* TB/840
M. S. ENSLIN: Christian Beginnings TB/5
M. S. ENSLIN: The Literature of the Christian Movement TB/6
HENRI FRANKFORT: Ancient Egyptian Religion: *An Interpretation* TB/77
MAURICE S. FRIEDMAN: Martin Buber: *The Life of Dialogue* TB/64
ABRAHAM HESCHEL: The Earth Is the Lord's & The Sabbath. *Two Essays* TB/828
ABRAHAM HESCHEL: God in Search of Man: *A Philosophy of Judaism* TB/807
ABRAHAM HESCHEL: Man Is not Alone: *A Philosophy of Religion* TB/838
ABRAHAM HESCHEL: The Prophets: *An Introduction* TB/1421
T. J. MEEK: Hebrew Origins TB/69
JAMES MUILENBURG: The Way of Israel: *Biblical Faith and Ethics* TB/133
H. H. ROWLEY: The Growth of the Old Testament TB/107
D. WINTON THOMAS, Ed.: Documents from Old Testament Times TB/85

Religion: Early Christianity Through Reformation

ANSELM OF CANTERBURY: Truth, Freedom, and Evil: *Three Philosophical Dialogues. Edited and Translated by Jasper Hopkins and Herbert Richardson* TB/317
MARSHALL W. BALDWIN, Ed.: Christianity through the 13th Century # HR/1468
ADOLF DEISSMAN: Paul: *A Study in Social and Religious History* TB/15
EDGAR J. GOODSPEED: A Life of Jesus TB/1
ROBERT M. GRANT: Gnosticism and Early Christianity TB/136
WILLIAM HALLER: The Rise of Puritanism TB/22
ARTHUR DARBY NOCK: St. Paul ° TR/104
GORDON RUPP: Luther's Progress to the Diet of Worms ° TB/120

Religion: The Protestant Tradition

KARL BARTH: Church Dogmatics: *A Selection. Intro. by H. Gollwitzer. Ed. by G. W. Bromiley* TB/95
KARL BARTH: Dogmatics in Outline TB/56
KARL BARTH: The Word of God and the Word of Man TB/13
WHITNEY R. CROSS: The Burned-Over District: *The Social and Intellectual History of Enthusiastic Religion in Western New York, 1800-1850* TB/1242
WILLIAM R. HUTCHISON, Ed.: American Protestant Thought: *The Liberal Era* ‡ TB/1385

SOREN KIERKEGAARD: The Journals of Kierkegaard. ° *Edited with an Intro. by Alexander Dru* TB/52
SOREN KIERKEGAARD: The Point of View for My Work as an Author: *A Report to History.* § *Preface by Benjamin Nelson* TB/88
SOREN KIERKEGAARD: The Present Age. § *Translated and edited by Alexander Dru. Introduction by Walter Kaufmann* TB/94
SOREN KIERKEGAARD: Purity of Heart. *Trans. by Douglas Steere* TB/4
SOREN KIERKEGAARD: Repetition: *An Essay in Experimental Psychology* § TB/117
SOREN KIERKEGAARD: Works of Love: *Some Christian Reflections in the Form of Discourses* TB/122
WOLFHART PANNENBERG, et al.: History and Hermeneutic. *Volume 4 of* Journal for Theology and the Church, *edited by Robert W. Funk and Gerhard Ebeling* TB/254
F. SCHLEIERMACHER: The Christian Faith. *Introduction by Richard R. Niebuhr.* Vol. I TB/108; Vol. II TB/109
F. SCHLEIERMACHER: On Religion: *Speeches to Its Cultured Despisers. Intro. by Rudolf Otto* TB/36
PAUL TILLICH: Dynamics of Faith TB/42
PAUL TILLICH: Morality and Beyond TB/142

Religion: The Roman & Eastern Christian Traditions

A. ROBERT CAPONIGRI, Ed.: Modern Catholic Thinkers II: *The Church and the Political Order* TB/307
G. P. FEDOTOV: The Russian Religious Mind: *Kievan Christianity, the tenth to the thirteenth Centuries* TB/370
GABRIEL MARCEL: Being and Having: *An Existential Diary. Introduction by James Collins* TB/310
GABRIEL MARCEL: Homo Viator: *Introduction to a Metaphysic of Hope* TB/397

Religion: Oriental Religions

TOR ANDRAE: Mohammed: *The Man and His Faith* § TB/62
EDWARD CONZE: Buddhism: *Its Essence and Development.* ° *Foreword by Arthur Waley* TB/58
EDWARD CONZE: Buddhist Meditation TB/1442
EDWARD CONZE et al, Editors: Buddhist Texts through the Ages TB/113
ANANDA COOMARASWAMY: Buddha and the Gospel of Buddhism TB/119
H. G. CREEL: Confucius and the Chinese Way TB/63
FRANKLIN EDGERTON, Trans. & Ed.: The Bhagavad Gita TB/115
SWAMI NIKHILANANDA, Trans. & Ed.: The Upanishads TB/114

Religion: Philosophy, Culture, and Society

NICOLAS BERDYAEV: The Destiny of Man TB/61
RUDOLF BULTMANN: History and Eschatology: *The Presence of Eternity* ° TB/91
RUDOLF BULTMANN AND FIVE CRITICS: Kerygma and Myth: *A Theological Debate* TB/80
RUDOLF BULTMANN and KARL KUNDSIN: Form search. *Trans. by F. C. Grant* TB/96
LUDWIG FEUERBACH: The Essence of Christianity. § *Introduction by Karl Barth. Foreword by H. Richard Niebuhr* TB/11
KYLE HASELDEN: The Racial Problem in Christian Perspective TB/116

MARTIN HEIDEGGER: Discourse on Thinking. *Translated with a Preface by John M. Anderson and E. Hans Freund. Introduction by John M. Anderson* TB/1459

IMMANUEL KANT: Religion Within the Limits of Reason Alone. § *Introduction by Theodore M. Greene and John Silber* TB/FG

H. RICHARD NIERUHR: Christ and Culture TB/3

H. RICHARD NIEBUHR: The Kingdom of God in America TB/49

JOHN H. RANDALL, JR.: The Meaning of Religion for Man. *Revised with New Intro. by the Author* TB/1379

Science and Mathematics

W. E. LE GROS CLARK: The Antecedents of Man: *An Introduction to the Evolution of the Primates.* ° *Illus.* TB/559

ROBERT E. COKER: Streams, Lakes, Ponds. *Illus.* TB/586

ROBERT E. COKER: This Great and Wide Sea: *An Introduction to Oceanography and Marine Biology. Illus.* TB/551

F. K. HARE: The Restless Atmosphere TB/560

WILLARD VAN ORMAN QUINE: Mathematical Logic TB/558

Science: Philosophy

J. M. BOCHENSKI: The Methods of Contemporary Thought. *Tr. by Peter Caws* TB/1377

J. BRONOWSKI: Science and Human Values. *Revised and Enlarged. Illus.* TB/505

WERNER HEISENBERG: Physics and Philosophy: *The Revolution in Modern Science. Introduction by F. S. C. Northrop* TB/549

KARL R. POPPER: Conjectures and Refutations: *The Growth of Scientific Knowledge* TB/1376

KARL R. POPPER: The Logic of Scientific Discovery TB/576

Sociology and Anthropology

REINHARD BENDIX: Work and Authority in Industry: *Ideologies of Management in the Course of Industrialization* TB/3035

BERNARD BERELSON, Ed., The Behavioral Sciences Today TB/1127

KENNETH B. CLARK: Dark Ghetto: *Dilemmas of Social Power. Foreword by Gunnar Myrdal* TB/1317

KENNETH CLARK & JEANNETTE HOPKINS: A Relevant War Against Poverty: *A Study of Community Action Programs and Observable Social Change* TB/1480

LEWIS COSER, Ed.: Political Sociology TB/1293

ROSE L. COSER, Ed.: Life Cycle and Achievement in America ** TB/1434

ALLISON DAVIS & JOHN DOLLARD: Children of Bondage: *The Personality Development of Negro Youth in the Urban South* || TB/3049

ST. CLAIR DRAKE & HORACE R. CAYTON: Black Metropolis: *A Study of Negro Life in a Northern City. Introduction by Everett C. Hughes. Tables, maps, charts, and graphs* Vol. I TB/1086; Vol. II TB/1087

PETER F. DRUCKER: The New Society: *The Anatomy of Industrial Order* TB/1082

LEON FESTINGER, HENRY W. RIECKEN, STANLEY SCHACHTER: When Prophecy Fails: *A Social and Psychological Study of a Modern Group that Predicted the Destruction of the World* || TB/1132

CHARLES Y. GLOCK & RODNEY STARK: Christian Beliefs and Anti-Semitism. *Introduction by the Authors* TB/1454

L. S. B. LEAKEY: Adam's Ancestors: *The Evolution of Man and His Culture. Illus.* TB/1019

KURT LEWIN: Field Theory in Social Science: *Selected Theoretical Papers.* || *Edited by Dorwin Cartwright* TB/1135

RITCHIE P. LOWRY: Who's Running This Town? *Community Leadership and Social Change* TB/1383

R. M. MACIVER: Social Causation TB/1153

GARY T. MARX: Protest and Prejudice: *A Study of Belief in the Black Community* TB/1435

ROBERT K. MERTON, LEONARD BROOM, LEONARD S COTTRELL, JR., Editors: Sociology Today: *Problems and Prospects* || Vol. I TB/1173; Vol. II TB/1174

GILBERT OSOFSKY, Ed.: The Burden of Race: A Documentary History of Negro-White Relations in America TB/1405

GILBERT OSOFSKY: Harlem: The Making of a Ghetto: *Negro New York 1890-1930* TB/1381

TALCOTT PARSONS & EDWARD A. SHILS, Editors: Toward a General Theory of Action: *Theoretical Foundations for the Social Sciences* TB/1083

PHILIP RIEFF: The Triumph of the Therapeutic: *Uses of Faith After Freud* TB/1360

JOHN H. ROHRER & MUNRO S. EDMONSON, Eds.: The Eighth Generation Grows Up: *Cultures and Personalities of New Orleans Negroes* | TB/3050

ARNOLD ROSE: The Negro in America: *The Condensed Version of Gunnar Myrdal's* An American Dilemma. *Second Edition* TB/304

GEORGE ROSEN: Madness in Society: *Chapters in the Historical Sociology of Mental Illness.* | *Preface by Benjamin Nelson* TB/133

PHILIP SELZNICK: TVA and the Grass Roots *A Study in the Sociology of Formal Organization* TB/123

PITIRIM A. SOROKIN: Contemporary Sociological Theories: *Through the First Quarter of the Twentieth Century* TB/304

MAURICE R. STEIN: The Eclipse of Community *An Interpretation of American Studies* TB/112

FERDINAND TONNIES: Community and Society *Gemeinschaft und Gesellschaft. Translated and Edited by Charles P. Loomis* TB/111

SAMUEL E. WALLACE: Skid Row as a Way of Life TB/136

W. LLOYD WARNER and Associates: Democracy in Jonesville: *A Study in Quality and Inequality* || TB/112

W. LLOYD WARNER: Social Class in America *The Evaluation of Status* TB/101

FLORIAN ZNANIECKI: The Social Role of the Man of Knowledge. *Introduction by Lewis A. Coser* TB/137